Strange Women
and Other Strangleholds

**An African, Christian Memoir of Marriage,
Divorce, and Survival**

Nena Ndioma

© 2015 Nena Ndioma

First published 2015 by
StorySheWrote Publishers Limited
Ellicott City, MD
USA
storyshewrotemedia@gmail.com

ISBN 13 - 978-0692509982

ISBN 10 - 0692509984

Praise for *Strange Women*

***

"In this beautifully written true story, Ndioma brings refreshing openness to her personal journey of surviving divorce without compromising her faith or her feminism. The book is a deeply intelligent display of women's liberation derived from expressing socially taboo feelings and vulnerabilities."

Sylvia Tamale, Professor of Law, Makerere University

"Nena Ndioma vividly describes her experiences as an African, Christian woman at the spinning confluent point where conflicting forces of marital betrayal, infidelity, tradition, religiosity, male chauvinism, taboos, societal stigma on divorce, and its consequences, converge on her. It is a story of hostages and escapes by a woman totally determined to break all the rules as her price for freedom. In the end, Nena Ndioma is a victor and not a survivor.

Reverend Emmanuel Baba-Lola, Rector, Rabboni Bible School and General Editor, The Confessional Prayer Bible

"Intensely personal, incredibly brave, unapologetically truthful, and beautifully written; Ndioma's memoir about divorce and the African Christian woman is a much needed intervention which all African couples interested in living honestly, respectfully, lovingly, and with God—as well as the people that care about them—should read."

Nwando Achebe, Professor of African and Gender History and Editor-in-Chief, Journal of West African History, Michigan State University

"A story with brilliant insights by a wise, caring and wonderful woman. A timely story. Nena Ndioma's story gives voice to the reality of many women's lives. It is a story of incredible courage, in naming the truths of married and divorced life and in demanding an interrogation of masculinity and femininity."

Jacinta Muteshi, Pioneer Chair, National Commission on Gender and Development, Kenya

"*Strange Women* is the story of one woman's courageous struggle to navigate a course to freedom, while honoring Christian morality and its primary ethic of love. Frankly and revealingly written, it is a book that will inspire and empower the legions of women suffering in silence to imagine life beyond their pain."

Amina Mama, Professor in Women and Gender Studies, University of California, Davis

"This is an important publication that lays out a brave, thoughtful pathway for modern Christian African women to constructively deal with the harrowing experience of divorce. As the essays here illustrate, Christian women must boldly insist on spousal accountability, firmly reject spousal failings as the price one pays for being married, and embrace God's love for them and their children by transcending fears of standing strong."

Nkiru Nzegwu, Professor of Africana Studies, and of Philosophy, Interpretation, and Culture, Binghamton University

"What *Strange Women* demonstrates is that … sometimes, [divorce] is the best way for couples and their children to recover … and grow in self-esteem with mutual respect."

Biko Agozino, Professor of Sociology and Africana Studies, Virginia Tech

Readers' praise for Strange Women

***

"I just wanted to say I read every single [essay] you have written and it did two things for me: I can almost make sense of my parents' failed marriage, and can see clearly some things I have to work on in mine … Bless you!"

"[Nena Ndioma] is truly a gifted writer...a refreshing new voice. … [S]he tells my story (and indeed that of so many other women). I am a divorced, Christian, African woman, and I must confess that I couldn't tell the story of my own journey better than she does."

"You have given me some very serious food for thought ..."

"Keep up the writing. It is blessing many."

"I love the way you write. You have a way of drawing your readers into the subject matter and keeping them glued to what you are saying. I would stay up all night reading you. … Please keep writing; it is therapy for you and a fantastic reading experience for me."

"Many women will be helped by your intimate honesty!! I wish there were such things to read when I was going through my [divorce] ordeal almost ten years ago."

"I am always moved by your writing."

"Such powerful sharing, and the wisdom you've gained along the way is so inspiring to us who are still trying to come up for air."

"You have a way … [a] visceral, deep understanding, but also the ability to teach others. You. Break. It. Down."

"You write the thoughts that I think …"

"God bless your heart … for these very important life skills. I am now better equipped with the tools to have a better relationship in future."

"Thanks for answering the call to write."

"There are lessons to be learnt [from *Strange Women*] regardless of your stage in marriage. To be honest, I have stolen nuggets of your wisdom and applied them to my 'happily married' life (note the quotation marks; no one is happy all the time). Some might question why I would be interested in a book about divorce, but I would counter, 'Why would I not?' There, but for the grace of God, go I. I'll take learning wherever I can get it. And if there is wisdom to be found in the memoirs of an African, Christian, divorced woman … then I'm going to find it, so help me God."

To the memory of my father

This is a work of creative non-fiction. It reflects the author's present recollections of her experiences over a period of years. Certain names and identifying characteristics have been changed or omitted, and certain individuals are composites. Dialogue and events have been recreated from memory, and, in some cases, have been compressed to convey the substance of what was said or what occurred. Although the conversations in the book all come from the author's recollections, they are not all necessarily written to represent word-for-word transcripts. Rather, the author has retold them in a way that evokes the feeling and meaning of what was said, and in all instances, the essence of the dialogue is accurate. A few excerpts have been fictionalized in varying degrees, for various purposes.

*Remember your journey from Shittim to Gilgal, that you may
know the righteous acts of the Lord*
(Micah 6: 5, NIV).

Contents

FOREWORD

At the core of the Christian faith is the call to love.

When I was asked to write this foreword, I thought about what it was that drew me to Nena Ndioma's words in this memoir, and as I considered it, I realized that it was the essence of love that is reflected throughout the writings.

Ndioma shares her experience of marrying a man and divorcing him. She shares openly with uncommon authenticity. She questions, she ponders, she accepts, and through it all, I believe she comes to love herself and perhaps even her former spouse in a way that many people may not understand.

The book is called *Strange Women and Other Strangleholds*. At first glance, you may believe that this is a book that will be filled with anger and bitterness, because generally when a divorce happens, that is all that is left. When a 'Strange Woman' and other kinds of 'strangleholds' come into a wife's home and destabilize it, usually the wife is left broken and wounded, but this book is not about that. It is a book about healing and acceptance. It is about finding your power through releasing your pain. It is a book about seeing the divinity that is wrapped up in the humanity of each individual.

Nena Ndioma calls us to a deeper understanding of life and love. Each story shared is so beautifully written, it pulls you into the scene. Often, you can feel the emotion in the author's heart as you read ... more than once, I was moved to tears or laughter.

This book is not for divorced women. It is not even for women. It is for everyone. For husbands, to have a deeper understanding of the inner workings of a woman's heart. For men, to see the possibilities that connection brings. For wives, to learn more about loving from a woman who had to let go. For women, to see how love can be perfected when we fall off the pedestal.

And through it all, there is God. With every page you turn in the book, there He is, because He is and always will be. Nena Ndioma shows us the power of her faith, because her faith leads her into His presence and in His presence, no matter what, there is fullness of joy.

I am one of the people who have had the privilege of connecting with Nena. In fact, if I may brag, I was one of the people that encouraged her to write her book. I believe that she is one of the new voices that will transform our world and I am honored to invite you to read this book. I pray that it touches your heart as it has mine, and that you are moved to reflect in a new way on your own life and the way you love.

Ekene Onu
Author, *The Mrs. Club*

Preface

Why this book was necessary

I started writing this book for one reason and finished writing it for another.

When I began writing it, I was a married Christian woman from Nigeria going through a divorce in Kenya. Writing was cheaper than therapy. Writing *was* my therapy. I needed to talk in order to heal and so I had talked to whoever cared to listen, trying to make sense of what had occurred in my marital life. I learned that you can only talk so much to your family, friends, and other loved ones without sounding like a broken record. After a while, you begin to sense that your 'talking time,' as a person desperate to heal, is up. Writing picked up where others left off.

With the passage of time, I became a divorced Christian woman. My reason for writing necessarily evolved at that stage. I still found writing therapeutic, but that's not the only reason for which I wrote. Looking back, I now realize that, subconsciously, I wrote to create 'elbow room' for myself and others like me – in the Church, in Africa – Christians that just happened to have experienced divorce. I wanted to emphasize that there is enough room for us, too – for us and our realities.

One of the first books I read after I came to the decision to file for divorce was Stacy Morrison's *Falling Apart in one Piece*: *One Optimist's Journey Through the Hell of Divorce*. As this author put it: 'My family and friends had gone with me on this journey as far as they could go. I would have to go the rest of the way on my own.'

This book represents 'the rest of the way' for me. It has afforded me the luxury of having an endless conversation with myself, fostering one layer of healing after the other. It has allowed me to say as much or as little as I have wanted, when I have wanted, when I have needed to. The book is part of a process that has helped me make sense of the demise of my Christian marriage, and in so doing, create closure for myself.

It began as a collection of memoir-based essays on my laptop. It began entirely for me and no one else. I discovered that if talking was therapeutic, there was also something incredibly restorative about putting things down on paper. And then I began to share the essays with my sister and she encouraged me to start a blog, patiently walking me through the process of setting one up. And then, I started getting comments on the blog from people I had never met and probably never will. And I realized that the issues I was writing about, which I thought were all about me, actually had a much broader application. The issues pertained to other women, too, and the larger society. I occasionally wondered why none of the books I had found about other women's divorce experiences were by African women like me. And I kept writing.

One of the earliest blog posts I wrote was entitled 'Strange Women.' I wrote it right after a church conference during which the Christian women in attendance prayed against 'strange women' – that is, women with whom their husbands were already romantically involved, or with whom they could potentially end up in extra-marital affairs. I was fascinated by this particular prayer angle and later discovered that it is actually quite common among African, Christian women. I soon noticed that some of the most popular internet searches that brought women to the blog contained words such as 'prayers against the strange women in my husband's life.' As I write this, the most recent visitor to the blog arrived from East Africa by entering the following words into her search engine: 'prayer bullets to eliminate the strange women.' Another visitor arrived on the blog from North America a few minutes before this, after using the search words 'prayer points against husband snatchers.' Similar search words have brought, and continue to bring, what I'm presuming are African women, from literally all over the world, to the blog. As a result, the 'Strange Women' essay was the number one post on the blog for a long time.

Although I believe deeply in prayer, I grew concerned by what I saw as the immense amount of pressure that Christian women seemed to be putting on themselves to ensure their husbands' faithfulness (as if ensuring this were their mandated role, or actually possible). It occurred to me that these actions represented a sort of 'stranglehold,' for lack of a better term – one that could potentially lead to the asphyxiation of many important phenomena: of one's joy, peace, and self-esteem; of critical, practical actions that could actually save a marriage; and, finally, of oneself. While I have never personally prayed the 'Strange Women' prayer, I have definitely experienced my share of 'strangleholds' in different forms, and in this book, I have not been shy about revealing and dissecting almost every one of them. Nearly every chapter in the book showcases a mindset, a belief, an attitude, or an action, that represents a potential 'stranglehold' which inhibited my own marriage from remaining strong, or which could have served as a stumbling block during my transition to, and in the aftermath of, divorce.

Employing the medium of writing, I 'remember my journey' (Micah 6: 5, NIV) through marriage and, ultimately, to divorce, as an African, Christian woman. My hope is that, by reading about my experiences and memories, other professing Christians in my part of the world will become more comfortable with the idea of telling the truth – will realize that it's okay to tell the truth about the unexpected ugliness that sometimes creeps up in all of our lives. By telling the truth myself, I also hope to 'spark a process' by which African churches and African society at large can deal with divorce more honestly, astutely, compassionately, and effectively. Along this journey, I have found myself continually problematizing divorce – revealing it for the immensely complex, multi-dimensional concept that it is. Hopefully, this process will be useful for others that are in the same place as I was when I started writing, and for the loved ones in their lives. Hopefully, it will help us all refrain from oversimplifying the issues that often lead to divorce, so that our solutions to these predicaments can be better thought-out and more practical and successful.

I have to warn you, though: the book is not written in chronological order by any means. I write about whatever comes to me, whenever it comes. This is a healing process, and if there's one thing I've learned, it's that healing can often be haphazard.

For the lips of a strange woman drop as an honeycomb, and her mouth is smoother than oil: But her end is bitter as wormwood, sharp as a two-edged sword. Her feet go down to death; her steps take hold on hell. Lest thou shouldest ponder the path of life, her ways are moveable, that thou canst not know them. Hear me now therefore, O ye children, and depart not from the words of my mouth. Remove thy way far from her, and come not nigh the door of her house: Lest thou give thine honor unto others, and thy years unto the cruel: Lest strangers be filled with thy wealth; and thy labors be in the house of a stranger; and thou mourn at the last, when thy flesh and thy body are consumed (Proverbs 5: 3-11, KJV).

Strange Women

The large room was packed full of African women drawn from various countries. This was our time to flee from our daily responsibilities and come together for a couple of days to be refreshed in God's presence. God knows we needed it. As Christian women, we often find ourselves pulled in multiple directions all at once – by church positions and responsibilities, husbands, children, careers, running a clean and peaceful household (with food in it) ... The list is endless – and every year, in my experience, just gets busier.

A one-hour prayer session began. The usual prayer topics I've come to expect at this sort of gathering. We prayed for our children, for our homes, for our health, for our spiritual lives, about family finances ... As we dwelt on these topics, the prayer in the room was collectively maintained at a nice, polite, even tempo.

And then, we were led in a prayer to 'unseat the strange woman' in our husbands' lives.

This prayer point had a poetic ring to it, I thought, as I turned the phrase around in my mind ... *unseating the 'strange woman'*.

I fought to hide a smile as the phrase suddenly seemed comical to me. It brought to mind an amusing image of a woman dramatically falling off a chair.

The Bible makes several references to this 'strange woman' (Proverbs 2:16, KJV), who 'flattereth with her words' (vs. 16); 'which forsaketh the guide of her youth, and forgetteth the covenant of her God' (vs. 17); whose 'house inclineth unto death, and … paths unto the dead' (vs. 18). The Bible also solemnly warns that 'None that go unto her return again, neither take they hold of the paths of life' (vs. 19).

The point was to pray against women who were serving (or who could potentially serve) as a distraction to the husbands of the Christian women represented in the room, who were coming in and invading Christian households, who were appearing on the scene and snatching women's husbands away.

The tempo of the prayers in the room immediately shifted into a frenzy that rose until the room was literally shaking. Women around me screamed, cried, yelled. I could sense some fighting physically with the air, contending against invisible strange women. Others clapped their hands forcefully, and stomped their feet in anger and indignation, binding the 'strange woman,' and commanding the grip of this mysterious, evidently powerful, and seductive woman on their husbands to be released.

I eventually found myself weeping on the inside in reaction to all I could hear and feel around me, my eyes tightly closed. My heart broke with every rising octave of the corporate prayer, as I witnessed ordinarily dignified Christian women morph into something I can't adequately describe.

Was this really happening? I wondered. *Were Christian marriages really this fragile? Had we really been reduced to this as women of God?*

I battled with waves of embarrassment brought about by this pathetic scenario. Although no longer married, I tried to keep myself focused on praying for God to protect and intervene in the marriages of those around me. I was jolted out of this prayer attempt, though, by multiple cries of "Every strange woman in my husband's life, I *unseat* you, *in Jesus' Name!*"

Where was this paranoia stemming from? What on *earth* has happened to Christian men? How did we get to this place? What is the church doing about all this? Surely, the solution can't be in yet another annual women's retreat to encourage faithful Christian women to hold on for one more year, for the next meeting, for the next visiting pastor, for the next prophetic word, or the next dab of anointing oil.

Who is working with Christian men? Why is there an assumption that men automatically 'know' how to be men, while women need constant, intensive Christian training? Where is the parallel annual men's retreat? The parallel men's prayer meetings and special Bible studies? Why does it seem like the preservation of a Christian marriage is solely a woman's burden to bear? Is it all about a never-ending exercise of praying against other women (as someone once asked, "How many strange women will you pray away?"), or do we also need to deal with the reality that the husbands we are trying to 'protect' are sometimes the actual predators in these illicit liaisons?

It would be so refreshing to see a room full of African, Christian men crying out to God for their wives and children, rebuking 'strange men,' and crying out to Him to establish them as true men of God.

I was heartbroken that it had come to this. Heartbroken because I instinctively knew that these same devout women would return for this same retreat the following year and pray just as fervently over this same issue all over again.

Does the solution lie in intercessory prayer, I wondered, or in finally making men a major project of the church?

Another approach I've seen Christian women rely upon to protect their marriages involves shunning their unmarried peers. I could never understand this approach, as it has always seemed really un-Christ-like to me. After an unmarried friend of mine 'took up' with my former spouse, I finally 'got' it (☺), but I still didn't (and don't) embrace the mentality. If I have to live in perpetual fear of my Christian spouse's infidelity, then there's a problem.

If this is what it takes to keep a Christian marriage together, then what's the point of marrying a believer (not that I'm even remotely suggesting that a Christian shouldn't, but you have to wonder …)? Why should a Christian woman have to invest so much time offering prayers meant for the 'unsaved'?

If we're not ready to invest time preparing men to be Christian husbands, then there's no point emphasizing to Christian women that they must marry believers – because if we don't prepare a generation of believing husbands … then … there *are* none.

4

'Except for marital unfaithfulness ...'

*The bravest, and best, thing Chris did when he said goodbye
is that he didn't wait until we had nothing left.
He didn't have the affair that obliterated our relationship,
sweeping all the complicated truths of our marriage
under the rug.*
— Stacy Morrison (author of *Falling Apart in one Piece*:
One Optimist's Journey through the Hell of Divorce), whose
ex-husband initiated the dissolution of their marriage, in
which no infidelity was involved.

There are a million 'little' things that typically lead to the end of a marriage and they are so hard to put into words. Most people with a marriage experience should be able to relate to this fact, I think. If you are married, or ever have been, you know that a marriage could be 'over' even while it still exists. Some marriages were dead and buried long before any actions toward divorce were ever even contemplated. Others 'survive' in their dead state, until the very end, giving off a semblance of marital success, both to on-lookers and to the married couple concerned.

Then again, some marriages really do triumph. Despite their imperfections (since nothing is ever perfect), the two individuals involved fight to keep the marriage alive, *insist* that it live, breathe, and remain authentic. This is what we all hope for.

In my case (unlike Stacy Morrison's), there were multiple affairs.

I suppose that, in the eyes of some in the Church, this gives my divorce legitimacy. After all, marital unfaithfulness is a deal-breaker, according to Jesus. As He once said, 'I tell you that anyone who divorces his wife, except for marital unfaithfulness, and marries another woman commits adultery' (Matthew 19: 9, NIV). A spouse's unfaithfulness is therefore seen by some Christians as the only 'out' for those too weary to embark on the journey of marital resuscitation.

And yet, interestingly, the multiple infidelities, though shocking, mind-blowing, and painful, were not the deal-breaker for me.

"I can get over this," I would say to myself intermittently, with complete conviction.

"I can deal with the infidelity," I would say to him, when there was still a glimmer of hope for the marriage. "Look, I'm a Nigerian girl. I grew up surrounded by the realities of infidelity. I didn't expect this to be my personal experience as one Christian married to another, but I can deal with it. I can deal with the infidelity, but I can't deal with the lies."

Although the infidelity itself was a lie, I was fully prepared to address it. I do not believe that infidelity has to spell the end for all marriages, and, in the initial stages, I did not believe it had to spell the end for mine. My personal opinion is that infidelity can be addressed if the parties concerned are willing and able to be honest about it, and if both parties truly see it as an issue worthy of eradicating.

Ironically (and contrary to Stacy Morrison's presumption), my discovery of the infidelity swept all the complicated truths of our marriage *out* from under the rug and forced me to confront these truths for what they were for the first time in a decade of marriage. I could no longer trust completely, for I now had proof. The dust accumulated over the years of the marriage was now in plain sight before me. I could no longer be in denial – I now had proof.

As 'shocking' as this might be to the Church, I didn't get a divorce because of the infidelity, necessarily. Beneath the surface of the 'legitimacy' granted by marital unfaithfulness lie a slew of the 'real' reasons why the divorce happened.

It was as if I'd been in a deep sleep for a decade and was suddenly and rudely shaken out of my slumber. I was forced to consider the accumulation of years of being a 'good, Christian wife,' the years of series of attempts at trying even harder. I was forcefully confronted by the fact that it had all been 'in vain.' As I wrote to my sister some years ago: "I denied myself so much, and went along with so many things that never would have been part of my life had I not gotten married. What was I thinking? I cringe to think of some of the things I allowed."

For all the times I was selfless; for all the times I cried and prayed in bewilderment over a man that sometimes acted as if he was unfeeling and made of stone; for all the times I stood up for things that didn't make sense in order to 'stand by my Christian man'; for all the times I tolerated careless decisions and endured the painful repercussions of these decisions in a bid to let the man 'lead' as a Christian husband; for all the embarrassment I had to endure over ruined relationships because I believed in the man I married, and would rather side with him than anyone else; for all the times I was left on my own to care for two small children and juggle a stressful job for months on end (the longest being eight months, during which I was pregnant), telling myself I was supporting my husband in achieving his dreams, and that it would all pay off some day; for all the times I cooked up a storm – special meals for my husband, whom I rarely got to see, and whom I so wanted to please; for all the times I tried to please every which way I knew how and came up against a brick wall … for all these reasons and more, and the fact that his apparent lack of remorse for the affairs devalued all my efforts, I filed for divorce.

Although the affairs did not in themselves lead to the obliteration of the relationship, the lies and falsehood that it took to sustain and protect them served as a major eye-opener for me. I suddenly realized that I deserved better. Not necessarily a better partner, but certainly a better situation.

I deserved better – even if it meant being by myself.

On being a martyr

My in-laws begged me to stay in the marriage. Not because they didn't feel I was fully justified in leaving, but because most of them valued me as an in-law (bless their hearts) and truly believed there had to be another way. My mother asked why I couldn't just stay for the children – or for the sake of my mother-in-law whom I had grown to love dearly. My response was that the children hardly ever got to see their father, anyway. Prior to our separation, the children were lucky if they saw their father for a week, three times a year. His business in another country was always supposedly too pressing a concern to permit him to spend time with us, in another. After the separation, he barely visited once a year. How a divorce would make much more of a difference wasn't (and still isn't) clear to me.

I told my mother-in-law repeatedly that I would always be her daughter, my relationship with her son notwithstanding.

"Who will ensure I have a proper burial when I die? Who will mourn me properly?" she lamented.

I assured her she wasn't dying anytime soon and that when this eventuality did arise, I would perform the full duties of a daughter toward her, no matter what.

My mother- and grandmother-in-law were among the first Evangelical/Pentecostal Christian converts in their village. My mother-in-law is full of stories of what it was like when the missionaries first came to her village. With my interests in anthropology and historical-type things, I've always been fascinated by these stories. I've always considered my in-laws as devout, and I still do. I would say without a doubt that, before we decided to get married, getting to know his family members sealed the deal for me. I was thrilled by the prospect of marrying in to a family that had essentially walked with God for a couple of generations, and that were (and are) really decent, kind, and giving people. Church is a big part of their lives, as is really trying to live by what they believe God says in the Bible.

As a strong Christian family, I suspect my in-laws never really thought it would come to this. Some continually put forth the fact that "nothing is impossible with God" – the unspoken implication being that if our family didn't remain intact, then it was because I didn't try hard enough.

Indeed, nothing is impossible with Him, I conceded … but even miracles usually have to be *wanted*.

This rhetoric was not unique to my in-laws, though. I literally couldn't escape from it, surrounded as I usually am in my life by devout Christian believers. My counter-rhetoric had me sounding like a broken record, given the number of times I had to repeat it to different categories of well-meaning people (WMP):

WMP: "There's nothing impossible with God, you know. Just give it time. God Himself will intervene. In fact, this is not even a serious issue. I know of some very difficult marital issues that God was able to resolve – how much more yours?"

Me: "I agree: nothing is impossible with God ... but what if this is simply something that I no longer want? Even miracles have to be *wanted* ... right?"

WMP: (Pause) "Well, you just need to persevere. You need to have faith. If you have faith as small as a mustard seed, you can say to this mountain, 'Move from here to there' and it will move. Nothing will be impossible for you." [Matthew 17: 20, NIV]

Me: "I know I can. But what if I don't want to? What if I like my mountain exactly where it is? Why take the divorce as a failure of faith, rather than as a simple lack of desire? Why is one easier to accept than the other?"

WMP: (Silence)

Me: "Should I really spend my energy 'believing God' for something I no longer want? What if I just choose to believe God for other things instead?"

Well-meaning church folks pointed out that children without a father in their lives are less likely to thrive. I pointed out that even when the marriage was at its 'best,' my children's father was absent more often than not, busy trying to make his fortune. *What's the difference?* I silently wondered. My children probably saw their father no more than four to five weeks out of an entire year.

As a woman brought up by a father that was adored, revered,

and larger-than-life, the importance of fatherhood is far from lost on me. I could actually put together that sermon and deliver it myself. But there is fatherhood, and then there is the happenstance of being born male. One should not be confused with the other. The fact that one is male does not automatically translate to availability to occupy the office of a father. I would, and still will, do pretty much anything to ensure that my children's father plays the role of a committed father in their lives. But marriage does not necessarily ensure that this happens (as many a married woman can testify).

A Christian friend of mine urged me to "just ignore the man and let him be there. Just keep him there" – much to my initial amusement! I found this hilarious, but sad, too, as it revealed the realities of many Christian women who have resigned themselves to ignoring their husbands and allowing them to just exist as the men by their side.

But it also made me more sensitive to a vibe from some people who were facing their own marriage struggles (and who isn't?); a vibe that said: "Who does she think she is to want more, to expect more?"

"This is just the way marriage is – even for Christians," the vibe said.

"Who told you *we're* happy? What makes you think *you* deserve be happy? What makes you think you're better than any of us? What gives you the right to change course, to demand a different life?"

My parents, after all, were not 'born-again' Christians, but had a marriage that lasted at least 40 years. The marriage certainly had its own ups and downs, but they stayed the course and raised their children together. Who did I think I was to make a different choice? These and other social pressures led me to write the following in my diary: 'Everyone expects me to be a martyr. My crime is refusing to die.'

Of course not *everyone* had this expectation. If anything, I have been surrounded by so much moral support that it's unbelievable. But there was still this sense I got from others (though not in so many words) that I was expected to 'die to self.' This I had been pretty good at doing (in my 'humble' opinion) for years on end, without which the relationship never could have lasted as long as it did. In so doing, however, I was *dying* without even realizing it. I was numb and could no longer feel.

And then, one day, I realized that I actually wanted to live. I didn't want to be a martyr. I felt like a suicide originally willing to drown to death, who sinks contentedly to the bottom of a swimming pool ... and then, as reality sinks in, suddenly changes her mind ... and begins to thrash, and kick, and fight – anything not to lose consciousness, anything to stay alive.

My life – what I have left of it – suddenly became something precious that I wasn't willing to squander just to keep up appearances, that I wasn't willing to waste out of a fear of the unknown.

As I hunted around for other women's stories, I realized that this experience was not unique to me. Jessica Bram captures a similar experience beautifully in her book, *Happily Ever After Divorce: Notes of a Joyful Journey*. As she describes it:

One day, at age forty-one, with three young children, I took a terrifying, guilt-inducing leap. After years of unhappiness, I finally found the courage to get out of my marriage. It was hard, no question. Hard like childbirth, like building a skyscraper or perhaps demolishing one. As hard as any of the most formidable challenges I had ever faced—every college or graduate school degree, every major disruption, every relocation, every turnaround.

But then, as after childbirth, a glorious new life emerged— but this time, it was my own. After my divorce I emerged into sunlight, stunned and blinking. Disoriented, yes, and many, many times afraid. But only then did life begin. Only then did I start to piece together, for the first time ever, a life that had fresh air and laughter, challenges and triumphs. A life of outer joys, and for the first time, inner peace.

I am here to say that it can be done.

As a Christian, I am not here to 'promote' divorce. I wouldn't wish a divorce experience on my worst enemy. There is nothing glamorous about the destruction of a family, nor about the utter devastation that divorce symbolizes.

But I *am* here to say my life is precious.

I refuse to die.

What if I told you I have HIV?

What price does an African, Christian woman have to pay before her divorce can be considered 'justified'? Through my discussions with others, I've discovered that there actually *is* a price – a hefty one. In divulging some of my marital predicaments, which led to my filing for divorce, I received a myriad of what I consider to be incredibly fascinating responses. Responses that made me feel like I was trapped in a Nigerian movie:

Nigerian Movie, Scene I

'It's okay. As a Christian, you can forgive, as Christ forgave you your sins. There's nothing impossible with God.'

Why does divorce automatically signify a lack of forgiveness for many? The fact that I no longer want to share my life with someone, live and sleep with the person – the fact that it's no longer even safe to do so – *doesn't* mean I haven't sincerely forgiven the person.

Nigerian Movie, Scene II

'Just know that if you divorce him, you can never re-marry. You must be prepared to live on your own for the rest of your life.'

15

A favorite response of quite a few people. It always makes me wonder: What's the *real* issue here? Is the concern that I'm on my way to hell because I could potentially re-marry? Or is it that I will 'rock the boat' of the church 'culture' should I ever decide to re-marry? For some reason, I suspect the latter is the real concern. Like I said, absolutely *fascinating*.

Nigerian Movie, Scene III

'If you do find out for sure that any of the 'other women' have HIV, make sure you don't gloat.'

Most shocking of all to me. I was stunned, frankly, by the seeming lack of concern for my own health that this comment demonstrates. But in retrospect, I suppose it reflects our socialization as Christians detached from 'the world,' and therefore from its realities. The reality that a spouse's involvement with multiple sex partners can put a Christian wife at risk for all kinds of negative health consequences (including death!) is totally outside the conceptual framework of many Christian women. After all, God is the Lord, who heals us – and He will put none of the diseases upon us which He brought upon the Egyptians (Exodus 15: 26). As long as I'm faithful to Him, He'll be faithful to me (Psalm 18: 25), ensuring that no harm befalls me (Psalm 91: 10)....

As compelling as this line of argument might be to we people of faith, lately, I've met too many wonderful, devout, Christian women currently living with HIV (or now dead from it) as a result of their husbands' affairs to continue to be this naïve. In some African countries, over half of all new HIV infections are estimated to occur within marriage or in co-habiting relationships.

"My people are destroyed from lack of knowledge," God said (Hosea 4:6).

Do I believe that God heals today? Absolutely. All I'm saying is that I've personally met numerous Christian women infected by their husbands who are battling with managing the illness – and, for whatever reason, I'm yet to meet a single Christian woman infected by her husband who received divine healing in this area.

I'm sorry, but we simply can't continue to bury our heads in the proverbial sand on this one. If you have sex with an HIV-positive individual (including a Christian individual you happen to be married to) without proper protection (meaning the *correct* and *consistent* use of condoms), you're putting yourself at risk for contracting the disease – fasting, prayer, church position, Holy Ghost baptism, prophetic anointing, and Christian pedigree notwithstanding.

Nigerian Movie, Scene IV

'After all, nobody's perfect – not even you. Let him who is without sin cast the first stone.'

Huh?

See Scene III above.

Nigerian Movie, Scene V

'There's no problem – just make sure your spouse gets tested for sexually-transmitted infections. If he comes out okay, then you no longer have anything to worry about.'

This isn't necessarily true. An STI-free spouse is not an indicator of behavior change. If the behavior has not changed, then there are still health risks, and their current state of health says nothing about what the future state of their health will be. Being in this sort of marriage is akin to playing Russian roulette.

<u>Nigerian Movie, Scene VI</u>

Complete silence

Cross-country email communication with friends about this issue sometimes resulted in complete silence. I was a bit bewildered by this initially, and even a teeny bit hurt (after all, some of these ladies were really good friends). But then, I thought about it: You never know what the woman right next to you is going through. Being open about such a sensitive issue can have several different effects on other women: it could remind them about a similar experience of their own which they are yet to divulge to anyone; it could make them begin to wonder just how safe their own Christian marriages are; or it could make them completely uncomfortable around you. It could also make them rally around you with the utmost love, empathy and support. This has been my blessed experience. I know it's not the same for everyone, and my heart goes out to those who feel abandoned and alone right now. Just know that He is with you (Haggai 1: 13), no matter what.

Bottom line, there are many who won't have the slightest idea what to do with a Christian marital experience of infidelity, what to make of it, and what support to provide. We're all only human, after all, and I'm certainly not suggesting anyone should be an expert at this!

Nigerian Movie, Scene VII

Post script

I eventually came up with the 'perfect' strategy for dealing with strange responses about 'strange women.' I began to totally circumvent them by simply saying, "I'm HIV-positive now."

The responses to this false announcement have always been really dramatic. Somehow, the reality of a Christian woman suddenly having to live with HIV due to her husband's carelessness really dawns on other Christians when they're confronted (or think they're confronted) with a person in the flesh who has experienced this. After a minute of observing the usual shocked reactions, I then announce, "I'm just kidding. Thankfully, I don't have HIV. I just wanted to see what you'd say."

And, in that moment, there *is* nothing to say. People are generally silent and confused as they internally thank God for your health and ask themselves (I think) what they would have done if the reverse had been the case. I find that the judgment fades in the face of reality, and for a moment, one is able to reason outside of all the Christian jargon, and actually put themselves in your shoes.

HIV infection is a game-changer.

(Talk about casting the first stone ...)

Permission from my mother

*... Or, did anyone force you to marry him? Didn't you
choose him by yourself? You must stay married to that man,
whether you like it or not!*

—An African mother

F ew African mothers (bless their hearts) will ever encourage
their daughter's divorce. Mine is no different.

In general, most women and men tend to equate divorce
with failure. A divorce is often seen as synonymous with
a 'failed marriage,' after all. But I think my generation has a
teeny bit of an easier time of staring divorce in the eye than
my mother's generation did. While the women of my generation
have access to a wider set of statuses, for my mother and her
peers, being married *was* their definitive status. They had fewer
opportunities to *be* anything else, and so 'failing' in marriage
was not an option. It didn't matter what the marriage was like.
Infidelity, irresponsibility, violence, STDs, death – name it – it
didn't matter.

My mother once said to me, pointedly: "A madman for a husband
is better than no husband at all." She had been telling me about

some woman's struggles with an irrational (and possibly manic) husband. I threw my head back and laughed out loud at her assertion, amused and positive she was just being facetious. Then I noticed the more-serious-than-joking expression on her face and I stopped laughing.

"Do you *really* believe that?" I challenged her.

She stared fixedly back at me with her answer in her eyes.

Wow, I thought to myself.

Out loud, I quipped: "Well, that's easy for you to say since you certainly didn't have a madman for a husband. Ask the madman's wife what she thinks."

I've never had a particularly easy relationship with my mother. Now that I look back, I can see that this partly stems from the fact that while I'm a 'born' communicator, my mother's communication style is very indirect, and therefore difficult to decipher. Understandably, our communication styles clashed too often for us to get along terribly well while I was growing up. With the passage of time, we've gotten better at communicating – or, rather, at accepting that we communicate differently, and at (sort of) trying to meet each other half-way.

I broke the news of my divorce plans to my mother gently, but clearly and directly.

"Mummy," I said, "I've been separated for a while now, as you know."

I looked her in the eyes and shook my head: "I have no plans to get back together with my husband."

I paused to let this sink in.

I took a deep breath, and deliberately softened the pitch of my voice, hoping she would understand I didn't mean to hurt her: "I wanted you to hear it from me before you hear of it anywhere else. I've hired a lawyer in Nigeria. I'm filing for divorce, Mummy. I've already paid the lawyer half of the legal fee."

I broke the news over a period of weeks, repeating the same message several times to give her time to absorb and make peace with it. Each time, in her characteristic communication style, she shrugged it off like an uncomfortable shawl, nervously laughed a little as if to help take away the sting of the unpalatable message, assured me breezily that the marital situation would get better ... and then changed the subject.

I understood that this was a painful subject for any African mother to consider. My divorce, after all, would have an impact on her life, whether real or imagined. What would people say? What message would the divorce send to others about my family, about my upbringing ... about my mother?

Our family home is named *Ndi oma* Lodge. '*Ndi oma*' means 'good people' in my mother tongue. It's an appropriate name – given by my father, who was a good man, and who left behind the legacy of a good name, good children, a good family. Good people.

I married into a family of good people, too. Indeed, a poignant plea from my former spouse was that I reverse my decision in order not to blight the divorce-free testimony of his family.

I found this interesting – at least theoretically: the mentality that not getting legally divorced could somehow bestow some sort of mysterious blessing on the entire family and the generations to come, when we had already been divorced in every other way for years. I could see the parallels between this mind-set and my mother's, and I could understand it. We were 'good people,' after all, and these kind of things aren't supposed to happen to us. Besides, nobody wants their world changed, re-arranged, ruptured – not even me. But if leaving your world intact means that I no longer get to exist (but you do); if not rocking the boat results in my being erased (while you're not) … then there's something fundamentally unfair about that picture. I'm sorry for wanting to *be*, for wanting to exist so badly.

The very last time I conveyed the news of the impending divorce to my mother, I did so firmly, yet gently and directly. Finally forced to talk about it, she said (essentially), "Listen – these issues leading to your divorce are non-issues. They're no big deal. You want to hear about marriage? Let me tell you about marriage …" And she began to narrate a litany of the typical marital experiences of her generation.

She started out with venereal diseases and I interrupted her, saying in turn: "Mummy, the diseases a man's carelessness could give a woman in your days were mostly curable. Today, the disease a man's carelessness will give you can *kill* you."

There was a long silence as she considered this reality, perhaps for the first time.

That was the end of the conversation.

The next day, after work, I was lounging in bed, trying to de-stress. My mother appeared in my room and sat on the chair by my bedside. We watched TV together quietly for a while. And then she began a conversation. A monologue, actually, with a captive audience of one.

She began by asking me if I remembered a particular family. She tried to describe who they were and I only had a vague recollection. People from my village whom I hadn't seen in years.

"Do you remember their daughter?" she asked.

I didn't really.

"Their daughter had a baby with someone in the village who wanted to marry her. She said she didn't want to marry him. So she left the baby with her mother and moved to the city. Sometime later, they said she was sick – very sick. She was coughing. You know: 'malaria.'" She uttered this last word with cynicism.

"She came back to the village looking like a broomstick. She was very weak; very tired. They said it was 'malaria.' Before you knew it, she could no longer stand. She was always sitting on the ground. Before we knew it, she died. 'Malaria' killed her, so they said. But because of how she looked, people knew it was AIDS. She was buried outside the compound – in the bush. Her mother gave birth to her out of wedlock and she herself was not married, so she could not be buried within the compound. Later on, the baby – a fine boy – died."

She asked if I could remember another young woman from a family I should know better, but don't. She continued: "She went for her national youth service. When she got back, she fell very

24

ill. We went to visit her at home, and when she saw us, she began to cry – that she doesn't know what 'they' did to her where she went for her youth service. She did not realize everyone had already heard she had contracted HIV. Her mother said she had been bewitched – that one day, a strange animal was found on her door, signaling the bewitchment. A young girl – very pretty. By the time I got back home from the visit, I was told that she was dead. That same day."

The next evening after work, I found my mother waiting for me, seated on the same chair. As I slipped out of my work outfit and fished around in my closet for a change of clothing, she launched into another monologue – this time, a new story about another young woman in my village who succumbed to AIDS.

The evening after that, she was seated in my room yet again, this time in semi-darkness. I switched on the light and she welcomed me with yet another story with the same chilling theme. This happened for a full work week. Each time, I listened attentively, making all the right noises to let her know I was paying attention, but saying very little.

By the end of the week, I understood.

My mother, from a totally different generation – my mother, in her indirect, cryptic fashion – was releasing me to make the decision I felt was best for me. She was letting me know that it was okay. It was okay to upset her world, as long as it meant that I would be okay and healthy. For my undemonstrative, reserved, guarded mother, this was the closest thing to saying 'I love you.'

Thank you, Mummy.

The correct and consistent use of condoms

I had already been tested for HIV during each of my pregnancies, but with the unraveling of my marriage came the need to get tested yet again. There was a Voluntary Counseling and Testing (VCT) center around the corner from my house. I passed the large signs pointing to the place every day on my way to work, never thinking I would ever have a need to go there.

One day, I drove into the compound of the VCT center and walked into the unfamiliar building. It was on a weekend in the early evening. I was surprised to find the building practically empty. After a few minutes, I was assigned a VCT counselor. My heart sank initially, as the counselor's physical appearance did not make a great first impression. I had caught a glimpse of her as I walked into the building, and, frankly, had mistaken her for a janitor. She wore some sort of large overcoat which I had come to associate with the vocation, and a pair of slippers. She paced sluggishly from room to room and initially addressed me in the local language before I explained that I didn't speak it.

When she ushered me into a private room, though, I had to revise my first impression. Before my very eyes, she switched gears and suddenly took on the persona of a serious and experienced professional. She began by asking about the circumstances that prompted my visit. I gave her a summary of the story which, by this time, I had grown weary of telling. For a minute, she slipped out of her professional persona and became a regular, fellow Christian woman: she heaved a deep sigh, shook her head in bewilderment and said, "I don't know what's wrong with our men. The church has a lot to do – a *big* job to do." She then began narrating a couple of other Christian cases she had come across recently through her work to support her thesis that the church needed to wake up: a pastor's wife who tested HIV-positive and who (unable to believe the 'man of God' infected her) repeatedly begged the counselor to tell her how else she could possibly have gotten HIV; an eighteen-year old girl who came out positive, and was absolutely incredulous, explaining that she had only ever had sex with one person, and he happened to be a pastor; the complexity of trying to explain to a devout, Christian couple how they suddenly ended up discordant – one testing positive for HIV and the other, not – after years of marriage.

I had come into the VCT center boldly, matter-of-factly, and on my own. I just wanted to get the HIV test out of the way and map out the way forward, based on whatever the results showed.

"Why didn't you tell me to go with you?" a friend of mine later asked. "How could you have gone all alone?"

I was touched by this, and explained that it hadn't even occurred to me to go with anyone. I wasn't sure what the results would show, but I wasn't scared, either. Up to that point, I could never understand why many women I knew would prefer not to know their HIV status at all, feeling that the shock of discovering they were HIV-positive would send them to an earlier grave than if they remained unaware. My stance has always been that the sooner you know about it, the sooner you can start taking care of your health.

However, after a few drops of blood had been extracted from my finger by the counselor, a sense of dread enveloped me for the next few minutes as we waited together for the results. I was taken aback as I hadn't expected to feel any fear. I was either HIV-positive, or I wasn't. But I did feel scared all of the sudden, and different scenes from my life sped before my eyes like an old movie at what seemed like a hundred miles per minute. I was besieged by a kaleidoscope of memories: my children as sweet-smelling infants ... my graduation ... my traditional wedding ceremony ... my father's smiling face ... myself at the age of seven – carefree and skipping barefoot on the hot sidewalk in the summer ... an image of my sister lying on the floor weeping when our father died ... my siblings' shocked expressions as I imagined telling them I was sick ... my children ...

To distract myself from this unexpected fear, I allowed my eyes to wander round the little VCT room, examining the posters on the wall, and the items on a table, trying to keep my breathing even and to push down the feeling of doom.

My eyes finally settled on a large, ebony-black, *ugly* rubber column (or a 'penile model,' as it is referred to where I live).

"Is that a penis model?" I asked the VCT counselor (not quite knowing what to call it). She answered in the affirmative and I said, "You know, I've always heard about these things, but I've never actually seen one. In fact, come to think of it, I've never seen a condom demonstration before. Would you mind doing one for me?"

The counselor obliged and as she proceeded, I temporarily forgot about my impending test results. "First of all," she said, slipping back into her experienced, professional counselor persona, "before you tear open the condom packet, you need to look on the back of the packet to verify the expiration date."

"Wait a minute," I interrupted incredulously, "You mean condoms have an expiration date?"

She calmly showed me the expiration date on the one she was holding.

As I explained to her, I had never, *ever* known this. As a matter of fact, I had never, *have* never bought a condom in my life. I had always left that to my spouse. And since the lights where typically off during sexual intercourse, I know for a fact we never checked expiration dates.

I sat there, shaken by the level of my own ignorance.

"Before tearing open the condom packet," she continued, "feel it to ensure that there's still air in it – it shouldn't be completely flat. If it is, there's a problem."

Lastly, using the big, ebony-black, unsightly 'penis model,' she demonstrated how to put the condom on.

I watched in silent fascination.

She put it on, ensuring some space was left at the tip to keep the condom from bursting. I stared pensively at the penis model for a few seconds and finally said, more to myself than anyone else: "I'm honestly not sure that this is how we used it during our marriage. I honestly don't know. I never checked. I didn't know what to check for. It never would have occurred to me to check."

At the age of 36, after a decade of marriage and two children, I finally received my first condom demonstration; I finally knew how to put a condom on correctly.

During the marriage, I saw condoms as my spouse's business. My assumption was that any man would know how to use them properly. Memories of friends who talked about not bothering to use condoms because 'they always end up bursting anyway' swirled around my head. Our assumption is that men know how to use them ... but who taught them? Who teaches a Christian man to use a condom correctly with his wife? Certainly not the church. Who else, then? Where do they learn? *How* do they learn?

I shuddered at these thoughts – at how much of my life I placed in someone else's hands, at how little responsibility I had taken for myself.

The counselor's voice penetrated my thoughts:

"Your results are ready now."

With some effort, I reeled myself out of my reverie and back into the moment. I took a deep breath and looked.

I was okay.

"Praise God, praise God, praise God," I said under my breath with my eyes tightly shut.

I was one of the lucky ones.

About to burst

Sometimes, I feel like I'm about to burst. I suspect that the consequences of this feeling may be rubbing people the wrong way. I tend to feel like this in church, mainly; this need to speak my mind, to say what I *really* think, rather than just smile placidly and nod as if I have no critical thinking skills.

Yesterday, I think I was particularly eruptive as I tried to express myself during a church meeting. I'm now here trying to analyze why. I feel almost like I'm going through a 'rebellious teenager' phase late in life. And now that I think about it, I finally get why. I find that the reason is not even directly connected to the subject of discussion at the church meeting. It is deeper than that: I kept quiet for so long, in a bid to be the 'perfect' Christian wife, that now – now that I'm no longer married – I have this subconscious need to make up for lost time.

Here are just a few things I've always wanted to say:

1. I do not believe that Bathsheba's act of bathing (II Samuel 11: 2-5) was a deliberate ploy to tempt King David. She was simply taking a bath, like we all do, for goodness sake! She had no control over the king being able to spy her from the rooftop of his palace.

She was bathing wherever it was that women bathed in her day, after all. What was she supposed to do – bathe with her clothes on?

2. As much as I admire Queen Esther, I have great respect for Queen Vashti, too. Had I been in Queen Vashti's shoes, I wouldn't have obeyed, either, if my inebriated husband commanded that I be brought before a great banquet for the sole purpose of parading myself around for guests to admire my beauty (Esther 1: 1-22). Drunkenness is so unattractive.

3. I think it's dangerous to infer from the story of Abigail (I Samuel 25: 2-43) that Abigail was submissive to her 'surly,' 'mean,' and 'wicked' husband (I Samuel 25: 3, 17), and that Christian women in abusive marriages should therefore endure the abuse. I find absolutely nothing in this story that points to Abigail's submission to a mean man. If anything, Abigail in her wisdom went behind her unwise husband's back and did exactly what he blatantly refused to do himself (I Samuel 25: 14-19). By so doing, she saved her entire household.

Abigail called her first husband what he was. In her words: 'He is just like his name – his name is Fool, and folly goes with him' (I Samuel 25: 25). Her truthfulness did not mean she was not a submissive woman, however. Abigail knew how to submit and be humble. The point is just that you do not submit yourself to danger. When she went to plead with David to disregard her husband's blunder, the Bible says that she bowed down with her face to the ground and then fell at his feet (I Samuel 25: 24). And everything she said to David – a reasonable man – clearly showed her humility. After her first husband died and she accepted David's marriage proposal, '[s]he bowed down with her face to the ground and said, 'Here is your maidservant, ready to serve you and wash the feet of my master's servants' (I Samuel 25: 41). This was a woman who knew how to be submissive without subjecting herself to foolishness.

There. I said it.

Today, I say most of what I say to make up for all the times I should have said something, all the times I could have said something … but chose to remain silent. I speak up now for all the times I suppressed my 'true' self, believing I would be rewarded for it with a glorious Christian marriage. In the process, I'm probably becoming increasingly unpopular with some. While I understand this, I'm not overly concerned by it. I feel like the real me is being revived, dusted off, and brought out of the attic at last. This is what I used to be like before marriage: nice, but opinionated. If I had just stayed that way, maintained my authentic self, not doubted for a split second that I was 'good enough' just the way I was, not obscured my real self for 'spiritual' reasons, I would have warded off the wrong people from my life and attracted the right ones. A *big* lesson learned.

I'm finding it pretty liberating getting to know myself again; being pleasantly surprised to remember what I really used to be like, and to realize that that person never actually died. It's also liberating not to care too much about what anyone thinks, not to have a spouse's fragile reputation to continuously protect, not to censor myself …

Like I said, I'm like a rebellious teenager all over again!

How do you tell your church it's over?

I used the medium of writing to convey the news of my divorce to my church in Kenya, where I live, and to my family outside the country. It was harder to convey the news to my church. While my siblings got the news the day after I learned of it (through a call from my lawyer), I waited another week before broaching the subject with key church members. I spend a substantial amount of time with my fellow church members and leaders at least once a week. With the advantage of proximity, they left no stone unturned in trying to piece my shattered marriage back together.

It's a small, family church. A mix of people from several African countries. About 100 people are in attendance on Sundays, if that. And then there are a handful of about six couples or so who go above and beyond church attendance to really make the place a sustainable home for everyone else. Some of these couples are much older, and others are around my age. Several of these couples poured themselves into my life in ways that I cannot adequately describe. When our marriage was in crisis, they visited us. Repeatedly. They sat with us and took the time to draw us out so they could figure out how to fix things. Now, that

34

takes a lot of guts in this day and age when most people do their best to mind their own business. One lady, on her second visit to our home, said to me: "I've just come to sit with you. We don't have to talk about what happened. We don't have to pray. We can just sit here and cry together. I just want you to know that I'm here." And then she just sat with me for a couple of hours.

They invited us to their homes. Made meals for us to share together and prayed for us. One emergency prayer and reconciliation meeting lasted five good hours, ending around midnight – and all the couples in attendance were very busy people.

They took the time to listen to each of us without taking sides. They let me express myself, regardless of their own personal opinions. Once, after a discussion I engaged in during a Bible study that focused on divorce, one lady said to me right afterwards: "Good. Talk it out. You need to vent. It's good that you said what you said. Don't hold it all in. Talk. Say what you feel." She was much older and had a solid marriage of over two decades under her belt. I had taken the opportunity to express my opinion on the subject even though it may not have been popular.

They spent their time and money on phone calls, reaching out to my then husband in another country and trying to encourage him not to give up on the marriage. They met with me after church – sometimes for hours, trying to convince me to keep my marriage together. They rooted for us until the end, firmly believing that, with God, all things were possible.

It was therefore really hard to share the news with them. I would begin crafting an email, and then end up deleting it. I did this several times before I finally took a deep breath, and hit the 'send' button.

Here, I share my letter to select members of my church family.

***

Dear Friends and Beloved Brethren in the Lord,

I trust that the year is treating each of you well so far.

Pardon me for relaying this message via email. I would have preferred to call each of you individually to convey this sensitive message, but since I've kept postponing it for various reasons (including travel, etc.), I thought it best to send an email before the month ends.

Fourteen years ago, on February 15, I took a leap of faith and got married. We were two young Christians, full of dreams, and with the best of intentions toward one another. Unfortunately, the union did not last and each of you is aware of the details. Ironically (and uncannily), our divorce was finally granted on February 15, exactly 14 years to the day of the marriage.

I wanted to let each of you know how deeply I appreciate your enduring concern over this matter, which each of you expressed in word and deed in ways that I will never forget. Each of you really continued to fight for the relationship, even long after I had no more fight left in me. I have no doubt that God will richly reward your efforts. My prayer is that as you have watered me and my family, may God Himself water you and yours in return. May everything that my marriage lacked be granted to each couple represented here in abundance. May every struggle that my marriage faced be a non-issue in your own unions. May God give each of you strength for your respective marriage journeys – strength to make it until the end. May your marriages be nothing but a source of pure joy – marriages in which you actually enjoy each other, rather than merely endure one another. And may your children have the privilege of witnessing what a true Christian marriage is supposed to be like. May that foundation lead them into their own stable marriages. In Jesus' Name.

I am grateful to each of you for always pointing me toward reconciliation, and for your genuine concern that I do God's will. The divorce was not a recommendation from any of you, or even from anyone else that I know. This was purely my decision. Thank you for pointing out the potential consequences of this decision, and for sharing your perspective on this decision, based on your understanding of scripture. Thank you also for respecting my decision, nonetheless.

Blessings to you all.

There's something wrong with my church

"**M**y husband and I have been separated for a while and there's no hope for reconciliation," I said pointedly to the Youth Coordinator in my church (whom I'll call 'Brother Faithful'), an older, committed, and respected brother in the Lord.

I said this in response to his request that I join the youth ministry/ department. I was already fully involved in one ministry in the church and didn't see how I could possibly find the time to fit in another. He explained that what the church really needed was an extra person to handle the pre-service Bible study for young adults, since he had been the only one performing this duty for a while, and he sometimes had to go out of town on business. Plus, they particularly wanted a female to get involved; to help handle issues arising in the lives of the young, unmarried women. My pastor had also approached me earlier with the same request, mentioning that a couple of other people in the church had recommended me for the role.

"What I mean is," I emphasized, not certain Bro Faithful completely understood me, "my husband and I are not getting back together."

He was sorry to hear this, and was already familiar with my 'story.' Still, he insisted that the separation was unfortunate, but neither here nor there. "I don't see what you did wrong, so as far as I'm concerned, that's not an issue," he said.

I stared at him with suspicion.

"Just give me some time to talk to Pastor about this," I replied, unconvinced. "You're asking me to join a sensitive ministry in which the young people might come to regard me as some sort of 'role model.' I know we need more hands in the youth ministry, but I just want to be sure that you all understand the implications of having me teach this particular class." We parted on that note.

This is how I was finally obligated to discuss my marital issues with my pastor's wife. My pastor was out of town, so I set up an appointment with his wife alone to ensure they were able to make an informed decision before the next Sunday, which was supposed to be my very first Youth Sunday School class.

I remember spending two hours in my pastor's office, with his wife, narrating the details leading to the end of my marriage for what seemed like the umpteenth time. Once I was done, I sat back and stared at her expectantly. She stared steadily back at me and simply said, "You must be a very good woman to have handled things the way you have."

I was mystified. Was that all she had to say?

I waited for a few moments, expecting her to make some additional comments. When she didn't, I said, "I just want to be upfront and let you know that the marriage is over so that you and Pastor can make a decision about whether or not you really want a divorced church member teaching the youth." I made sure I put stress on the word 'divorced.'

"That's not a problem," she said. "This is not about that. This is about you as a person. You as a person can teach this class. I know Pastor won't have a problem, either."

And so, the next Sunday, I found myself seated in the Youth class for the first time, teaching Sunday School to young adults.

Fast forward several months later, and there I was, immersed in a whole range of youth ministry activities, thanks to Bro Faithful, who kept pulling me into different events. "I thought I was only supposed to teach Sunday School," I protested. Bro Faithful laughed and said he was actually planning to have me 'take over' from him so he could devote more time to regional church matters.

"What?! No way, I'm too busy. In fact, I actually meant to talk to you to find out if you're sure you don't want to revise your decision. A series on marriage is coming up in the Sunday School class. Aren't you even remotely worried about having me handle that topic?"

"Why would I be?" he asked, with what seemed like genuine curiosity.

I thought this had to be some sort of a joke. My overall church is known for its conservatism and so I wanted to make sure that I avoided any surprises beforehand.

"Well, I know I told you in the beginning that my husband and I were separated, but since then, we've actually filed for divorce. Don't you think we should slow down on this youth ministry thing and think about what this really means? In fact, I need you to really impress upon Pastor that the marriage is really over so that he takes this into account."

"Oh, that's not an issue," Bro Faithful quipped. "In fact, I meant to tell you: Pastor told me to inform you that he wants you to be a member of the parish council."

"What?!" I burst out laughing in disbelief and genuine amusement. Were my church leaders well?

My peals of laughter were met by an offended silence from Bro Faithful.

I composed myself and apologized. "I'm sorry … I don't mean to trivialize this … This is just so unexpected. Why would he want me to join the parish council?"

"Because he and the parish council members think you would do a good job of making sure the interests of the youth are represented."

"Oh."

A little bit confused, I groped around in my mind for another argument, convinced that my church leaders hadn't really grasped the ramifications of involving me in all these areas.

"But you know me, Bro Faithful. Aren't you concerned that I'm a bit too opinionated to be part of a group like the parish council? And remember, I'm getting divorced. I don't want a situation where I'm unceremoniously pulled out of the youth ministry once my divorce is final. If my divorce will pose a problem for the church, please let me bow out gracefully now. The young ladies can still feel free to come to me if they ever need to talk, but I don't need this sort of visibility if it's going to be an issue later."

"You've been a blessing and a role model. A lot of the young ladies look up to you – do you know that?"

"But that's the point," I countered, "I don't want to be a role model."

Bro Faithful just laughed.

Clearly, there's something wrong with my church.

I've had friends that have experienced severe, blatant abuse in their marriages, only to be shunned and judged by their own churches when they decided to turn there for help. Committed, seasoned Christian women, who had served faithfully in their churches for years, only to be dropped like a hot potato in their time of need. I've seen friends forced to leave the churches they had always loved because of the lack of support once marital problems began. I've had friends shunned by their pastor's wives because they somehow saw their parishioner's need for support as some sort of threat to their own marriages. I know of many women that have been stigmatized by their fellow church members (mainly, other women) because only women with intact marriages were seen as having any worth, any rights, any place, any voice, any existence.

Why this hasn't been my own experience, is beyond me. Perhaps my church is just unique, one of a kind. Perhaps my church is just weird.

My church is definitely made up of a good number of solid, balanced, Christian brethren whom I greatly admire. But I suspect it's more than that. When I think about the Christian women I know of who have essentially been marginalized by their churches, I seem to notice one common denominator: a sense of shame.

As a result of this misplaced feeling of shame, they all seem to share the characteristic of not being fully open with their churches. They might provide their churches with bits and pieces of their story (if that), but never the full picture. They might tell their pastors about the infidelity, but hide the fact that they're regularly being beaten black and blue by their spouses. Or, they'll mention the infidelity, but not the fact that their spouse has contracted HIV. They might mention the economic neglect, but not the unfaithfulness.

Shame is an extremely potent emotion. It can be sensed by others, even though they may not realize what it is, exactly. I may be wrong, but there seems to be something about shame that inadvertently attracts disrespect. Shame makes people *small* – in their own eyes and in the eyes of others.

I'm not sure why I have never felt shame about my own marital situation, about why I have never had a problem speaking up about it. But I've noticed that being open and upfront often has a radical effect on people. It's all in the eyes. That is, you can literally see the eyes of women light up with surprise, then respect, then wonder, when they meet another woman that's sincere about her own life. The truth is really refreshing, I suppose. It would be great if we weren't so afraid to tell the truth as Christians.

Sometimes, the problem lies with our churches ... sometimes, the problem lies with us.

What if every Christian woman told the truth? (What a radical concept!)

Evil patterns

I've lived outside Nigeria for so long that I haven't heard or come across the phrase 'evil patterns' in a long, long time. The concept of 'evil patterns' is one that seems to resonate strongly with African Christians in particular. From my observation, there are at least two reasons for this. One has to do with scriptures such as Jeremiah 31: 29 (NIV), which suggest that, historically, children have had to bear the consequences of their parents' sins:

'In those days people will no longer say, "The parents have eaten sour grapes, and the children's teeth are set on edge."'

The idea of having to pay for the sins of one's forefathers holds considerable cultural resonance for many Africans. In the opinion of some, the fact that our forefathers were not Christian puts even greater pressure on us to unearth evil patterns in our bloodlines and deal with them in prayer. Culturally, there is no calamity without a cause – and these unwelcome evil patterns that often haunt us and seem impossible to escape are often pinpointed as the culprit behind our misfortunes. Understandably therefore, such patterns are often a focus of regular prayer.

I attended a prayer meeting recently that brought back ancient memories of the concept. One of the prayer points focused on the issue of 'evil patterns' that run in families, and divorce was specifically mentioned as one of these patterns. The instruction was for attendees to pray against such patterns.

As the fervency of this corporate prayer built up, my mind wandered and I found myself lost in thought. What evil patterns could I identify in my family? I dug around in my mind but couldn't come up with anything particularly unique to my family – i.e., anything that didn't occur in other families I knew of. Then I chided myself for embarking on a futile exercise. Nobody's perfect – and if I could accept this reality, why would I assume any family was perfect?

What about divorce, though? Could my divorce be an indication of the evil patterns besieging my family?

I guess it depends on how you look at it.

When my mother first heard about my appearance in court as part of the divorce proceedings, her initial reaction was to cry, although I had been preparing her for this eventuality, and had been keeping her abreast of the developments. As she cried softly on the phone, I told her to wipe her tears. Because my divorce is not something that 'happened to me,' necessarily. The circumstances leading up to it were 'visited upon me' in the sense that I had little control over them, yes. But the divorce itself was a carefully-made choice on my part. It was a choice I made about how I no longer wanted to live.

If I wanted to remain married, the 'marriage' was (and, I daresay, still is) mine for the having. I could have stayed married forever, actually. After all, to many of us, the content of the marriage doesn't matter. All that matters to most people is that you stay married, even if you're living divorced lives. And so, I very well could have chosen to remain in a dead marriage beyond redemption – and I'm sure this would have rubbed the overwhelming majority the right way. But it wasn't right for *me*, and I suddenly had the radical realization that I actually matter.

We were separated for four years before the divorce. I wonder if those years of separation (when, technically, I was still married) would qualify as an evil pattern, too. Or if the pattern is only in operation when there's an actual, legal dissolution of the marriage.

Or maybe the evil pattern lies in the choice I made to officially end my marriage. Perhaps, in my family, there's a propensity for women to make this sort of decision after years of stomaching things that shouldn't be part of a marriage in the first place. In which case, the evil pattern would reside in the tendency for us to make 'poor' life partner choices … in which case, this can't really be called 'evil,' but perhaps a lack of wisdom/discernment (or a mere lack of street smarts!) instead … in which case, even I can agree that we can find patterns anywhere we look for them, including in our families – but they're not always associated with evil … in which case I feel better now about not spending those few minutes in fervent prayer, but rather, 'unpacking' evil patterns – and in so doing, realizing what I *really* needed to pray about.

Not the same category

You and me no dey for the same-u category
You and me no dey for the same-u category
Not de same category O ...

— *Fela Anikulapo Kuti*

Our Women's Department in the church had been limping for a while and a meeting was convened to try and understand why. Less than ten of us sat together and took some time to think about how to respond to this question. How come this particular department wasn't thriving?

There was a two-minute-long, pregnant silence as we sat in a semi-circle, avoiding each other's gazes. I was a bit puzzled by the silence. This was not a difficult question. Did we honestly have no inkling of what part of the problem might be – no personal opinions about this – or were we all just too shy? Had we never thought about this issue privately before?

Two minutes were all I could bear, and so I asked myself why I, personally, rarely attended any women's meetings or events. I looked around at each of the women at this meeting and decided to speak up.

"Well, I just took a look around at the eight women here and I noticed something. Let's just go round the circle," I said, pointing to each woman one after the other: "Married; not yet married [single parent]; married; widowed; not yet married [single parent]; no longer married; married" – and, lastly, there was someone that I couldn't quite categorize because I simply didn't know the details of her situation.

I pointed out that those of us present represented the wider church. This is how diverse we were, if we really took the time to think about it. And so, if by 'women's' meetings, we really mean 'marriage enrichment' meetings, then we need to be clear and upfront about this so that potential attendees are targeted properly.

There's nothing wrong with marriage enrichment meetings. They are clearly important and sorely needed. But if we really want to reach a variety of women in the church, we have to pause and ask ourselves who they are and what their needs might be. The needs of other women have to stop being an afterthought – a last minute, hasty add-on of a few words (or a last minute adjustment to the meeting title), to hopefully cater to their needs.

The problem with this approach is that it insults the intelligence of those that the hasty add-ons were meant for.

When your needs are an afterthought, you know it. It shows.

Who says we *all* have to be in the same meetings *all* the time just because we're all women? That's another part of the problem, I think.

It's okay to say that we're different.

Sometimes, a small meeting for older women who have never been married, for instance (as opposed to a youth meeting which older, unmarried women are expected to attend, be enthusiastic about, and perhaps even grateful for), is exactly what's needed to do the trick. Sometimes, married women need their time together to hash out and pray about their own unique issues.

When 'general' women's meetings are the goal, though, a thoughtful approach is needed to focus on (as one married woman – the only other one that spoke up – said during this fact-finding meeting) 'those things that bring us *together*.'

How refreshing, I thought.

The truth is: we're not all in the same category. And that's perfectly okay.

Abracadabra

The Sunday School topic at church yesterday centered on marriage. As the lesson progressed in the young adults class, I could see the longing in the young people's eyes for an uncomplicated answer, an easy way toward ensuring they ended up with the right life partner – one who would ensure they maintained a joyful married life; one who would be there for the long-haul.

I explained that the solution lies in a combination of prayer and practicality. Prayer for God's guidance and wisdom is essential, but after praying, you have to do your due diligence, using the wisdom He has given. You have to accept the guidance that He makes available (by not ignoring the red flags He shows you because you're too much 'in love'; by being open to listen to the impressions of others that have loved you and known you much longer than your suitor has, etc.). Ultimately, you have to know how God speaks to you way before marriage – and you have to *listen* to what He impresses upon you when marriage time comes around – rather than ignore His voice and assume everything will turn out okay just because you 'prayed' and just because you're a Christian.

Not completely satisfied – still hoping to find the 'magic bullet' – a young lady in the class turned to an older woman with at least thirty years of marriage under her belt, who happened to be in the class, too.

"Can you give us some advice on what exactly we should pray about? What should our prayer points be, exactly, as we prepare to meet our life partners?" she asked eagerly.

The older woman being addressed thought about it for a second, and then wearily gave an answer, pointing out that every Christian woman wants a partner that knows who God is, can go to God in prayer, etc. These were, thus, examples of things to pray about.

The young ladies took down notes furiously as she spoke. They took copious notes during the entire class, come to think of it.

As I sat back and watched this scene, I silently blessed the young ladies and wished them well. My sister's long-standing argument also rang in my ears: "There's an element of luck in this thing," one of my sisters has always maintained. Although I disputed this when I was younger, the older I get, the more I'm tempted to agree with this assertion.

I think there are two things involved: you can either do your due diligence and respond to red flags as actual danger signs – or you can hope that 'luck' will shine on you.

When I search through my inventory of friends and acquaintances with happy marriages, I find that each person falls in either of these two categories. I have friends and acquaintances that got married way too young – before they even knew what life was about. I know of some who got married to their own converts not long after the conversion – something we were always warned against when I was a younger, unmarried lady. Some got married to obviously weak, not-too-committed Christians who suddenly 'sat up' where the things of God are concerned right after the wedding. Others ended up married to people they barely knew, with no real courtship to speak of. Although I'm certain some marriages born this way end up back-firing, each of the people that I have in mind have been happily married for years. Although my Christian world-view clashes with the notion of 'luck', I'm beginning to think there's *got* to be some element of luck involved, at least *some* of the time.

Depending on 'luck' in finding 'The One' is a precarious way to go, though, as luck is, by its very nature, unpredictable and unpromised. If I had to do it all over again, I would go for doing my due diligence. I would be much more business-like about it (which I find that men tend to do really well), doing my research to find out if partnering with this person would be a good 'business deal' or not – and if not, telling myself the truth about this – and honoring myself enough to listen to me (i.e., God within me).

If I had to do it all over again, I wouldn't stifle myself to keep the peace, or to squeeze myself into the portrait of the perfect potential wife. I would just be me, knowing that this would be more than enough for whoever is really supposed to be in my life for the long-haul.

In not insisting on 'being me,' I was complicit in the demise of my marriage. I thought that not asking too much of life, of my marriage, was smart. Safe. Brilliant. I thought not asking too much would ensure that I got everything. I thought it was my magic bullet.

I was wrong.

In my bid not to ask for much, not to be demanding, not to expect much, I gradually began taking on more and more responsibility in the relationship. I honestly thought that this sacrifice would solidify my place in my spouse's heart. That I would be paid back with gratitude and everything else that comes with it. I thought my husband would, as a result, 'arise and call me blessed' (Proverbs 31:28, NIV).

I see now that it seemed easier to me, at the time, to take on more and more responsibility, to do with less and less of him, than to confront the issues in the marriage that were eating me alive. It was easier to try and be Superwoman, managing on my own, than to talk everyone's ears off about our actual issues, until I found a real remedy. I see now that it was easier to be Superwoman on the outside, than to precipitate a process that would lead to a never-ending cold war between us. I preferred to be Superwoman back then than to contend with a cold war.

And so, behind the demeanor of the perfect Christian wife, standing by and submitting to her husband, hoping against hope that God would see me and rescue me like He did Sarah (Genesis 20) ... was a palpable fear. I was scared to death about the direction in which my life was headed. I felt like I was in a fast race car, spinning out of control – and I was not the driver. All I could do was sit in my seat, holding on for dear life, and pray like crazy for God to keep me safe. I essentially became lazy about my own life, without really realizing it. It was easier to try and juggle multiple balls in the air than to take the time to decide what I really wanted out of life and what I needed to do to get there. At least, with all my responsibilities, I had the excuse that I was too busy doing 'noble' things to think about myself. It was easier to believe that God would take care of it all, and that my only job was to be faithful to Him. As long as I took care of His business, He would take care of mine. Taking responsibility for myself was not in my job description.

Well … you know what they say about faith without works.

These are some of the things I wished I could have said to the young ladies in the youth Sunday School class.

I didn't, though.

I felt a tad guilty about possibly bursting their bubbles. I sat back admiring the beauty of their youth and told myself that they didn't need to have their innocence destroyed just because I chose to get divorced. I didn't want to be the one responsible for dimming the bright, hopeful light in their wide eyes.

They were hoping for a magic bullet, and who can blame them? We could all do with a little magic in our lives.

Did I marry beneath myself?

I've had people wonder about this before in regard to my previous marriage. I don't think there's a simple 'yes/no' answer to this question. In my mind, it only leads to a series of other questions.

When we talk about a person marrying beneath himself or herself, what are we really referring to? Are we referring primarily to one's own money or wealth, the money or wealth of one's parents, the social 'class' of one's family, one's level of education, one's character ... or all of the above?

My father would have given a blunt answer to this question. As far as he was concerned, I had selected a life partner who was beneath me, and he made this clear before the marriage. He wasn't the only one that thought so.

Back then, I was deeply intrigued by this concept and asked my father to elaborate. He didn't articulate what he meant beyond saying that my parents were highly educated and his were non-literate, and so, in a sense, I was choosing to 'start all over' – losing the gains my parents had worked hard to make. I didn't get it then and (to tell the truth), I still don't really get it now. 'It' (whatever it is) would have been crystal clear to me if I were marrying an uneducated person, while being educated myself. But this wasn't the case. The parents of the person I married may not have been to school, but they produced remarkably high-achieving children whose accomplishments rival those of my parent's children.

I guess I'm just of the opinion that, no matter who your parents were or are, you still have to prove yourself and make your own name in your own generation. Having the 'right' set of parents may or may not help you in this regard. Coming from the 'wrong' side of the tracks may or may not end up being the motivator that propels one to unprecedented heights.

A young person I know recently told me that she could never marry a 'poor' man, being from a relatively well-off family herself. Her point was that being raised 'poor' establishes a certain kind of psyche that the person concerned cannot escape from, even if they end up striking it rich on their own, or rising to a higher social 'class' – and she could foresee this as causing unnecessary problems in marriage. I admired and applauded her for doing her own thoughtful analysis on this issue at such a young age. I wish I'd been that 'street smart' in my early twenties. While I appreciate where she's coming from, I also know that strange mind-sets aren't the preserve of the 'poor.' If the 'poor' have ways of thinking, then so do the 'rich.' And either mind-set could come with its own problems.

I know of a really wealthy heir who doesn't have to work (and doesn't). Middle-aged, his life is spent traveling to exotic locations and doing only the things that he thoroughly enjoys. But his mind-set is, in many surprising ways, that of an impoverished man. He tends to be unusually (embarrassingly, even) stingy toward others, and (apart from the exotic trips), toward himself.

Who's to say exactly what effect money (for instance) has, and whether this effect is consistent across all individuals? What if in-born personality has the greatest effect of all, irrespective of who one is or what one has?

As I pointed out to my Dad at the time (with my idealistic, youthful self), he was once that young man whose parents were non-literate. But nobody remembers that now because of his own achievements – so why (and how) did it matter?

I don't claim to have any of the answers, but I do know that whatever occurred during my marriage could have happened even if my ex-husband's parents were royalty. We all know people with seemingly the 'right' pedigree who ended up making really horrible spouses.

Having said that, let me also say that Christianity absolutely does (or, at least, ideally should) level the playing field. Being a Christian will often mean that you will constantly engage with people from all walks of life – some 'above' you, some 'beneath' you, and some 'at par' with you. It also often means that you will tend to give each of these categories of people a fair chance when it comes to marriage. Our prayer is that, whether the person we end up with is viewed by others as 'beneath' you or not, let it not be because of their character. And if there are any other 'inequities' between the two of you, they should be carefully examined before you say 'I do.'

God's decision

How important is God's decision when choosing a life partner?

This is a question a young lady once asked me. The first thought that came to me was: *Well, it depends on what you consider to be 'God's decision.*

'Knowing God's Will in Marriage' is a topic that comes up every year in Sunday School at my church. We don't actually call it 'Sunday School,' but that's more or less what it is: an hour of time before the Sunday service to give congregants a chance to go over the scriptures and explore a particular issue. This year when it came up, I put two young ladies in the class on the spot by asking them how they knew they had chosen the 'right' major to focus on in college. One of them had just completed her bachelor's degree and I asked her to look back and tell us about her experience:

"Do you feel like doing a bachelor's degree in Economics was outside of God's will for you?" I asked.

"No, not at all," she said with complete conviction.

"Okay, so say more about that. How did you know you were supposed to study Economics and not any of the other half a million majors you could have chosen? I mean, you didn't start out as an Economics major, did you?"

She proceeded to explain to the class that she actually started out as a pre-med student. Her grades were great in her first year and all that, but as time went on, her class was taken through an orientation program to understand what the pre-med program would be like through the years, and to understand what a career as a physician is like. She suddenly realized that this wasn't the path for her. Again, her grades were strong and once you start pre-med, you don't wake up one day and tell your African parents that you've suddenly discovered you don't want to be a doctor. So she began to pray for God's leading and help. In the meantime, she noticed she was drawn to all her Economics and Math-type courses. She'd always liked and had been good in Math, etc., but she had sort of overlooked that in a bid to follow what seemed like the more glamorous path of Medicine. As she listened to her heart, though, she knew she needed to switch majors. After some weeks of committing the issue to God, she found the courage to break the news to her mother – a committed Christian with whom she shares a very close relationship. To her surprise, her mother mentioned that she'd been praying and had a dream that her daughter was an economist, so the news came as no shock to her. Today, she actually is an economist with no regrets.

The other young lady whom I asked the same question was pursuing her master's degree.

"How did you know you were supposed to study Communication?" I asked. "Or do you think you might be operating outside God's will?"

"No; I know I'm studying the right thing because I have a passion for Communication. It's never been a struggle for me. I've always enjoyed it and done well in it and I believe I'm on the right path."

My point is that the notion of 'God's decision' needs to be demystified. What do we really mean by that, anyway? It's not necessarily supposed to be a spooky concept. Why can't it be 'our' decision while we relax in the knowledge that God orders our steps and we have the mind of Christ – thus it's technically 'His' decision, too?

The process of choosing a life partner, in my opinion, is not much different from the process of choosing the right major for you. It's all about knowing yourself and your heart well enough to know when something seems or feels 'right' or not. It's about not ignoring that still, small voice that we all have within us – not suppressing it. It's about choosing Medicine over Economics (or Economics over Medicine) because you know how to listen to your heart.

Now, for some of us, this takes practice and a keen awareness of self. For me, it took far too long before I began to pay attention to this voice, or to my heart. I just didn't know any better. I'm from the generation that was taught (directly or indirectly) that God's speech usually manifests in 'spectacular' ways – through dreams, prophecies, words of knowledge, etc. I learned little about God's 'every day,' 'every minute' ways of speaking, which are critical to be familiar with since He lives in us and is speaking all the time.

I am sure God speaks often in 'spectacular' ways to some people; we all have different giftings, after all. But for most of us, it is through an inner *knowing* that becomes more familiar and easier to sense as we practice the art of paying attention.

When I was asked this question by the young lady concerned, I immediately started doing some calculations and I discovered that I have lived for a total of about 15,000 days on this earth so far. In my 15,000 or so days on this planet, I have had less than ten dreams in which I received crystal clear guidance on what I needed to do about a particular issue. If I were to depend on dreams alone to make decisions (or to decide what 'God's decision' is), I would have made alarmingly little progress as a human being. I also think that sometimes, we wait around to 'know God's will' via a dream, prophecy, and the like, because God may habitually speak to the people around us in that way. But our question to ourselves should be: *How does God speak to me?* If He hasn't regularly spoken to me in that particular way (e.g., dreams) about other things in my life, why would I expect that He would suddenly speak to me in that way just because I'm ready to get married? Just be you and let Him deal with you as you.

Whether we believe that the choices we are to make (about marriage and any other major decision) can only be made through an angel with a trumpet blast, or that mutual attraction and compatibility (or both!) are the ways to make such decisions, the fact is that the work of marriage remains the same. Exciting spiritual encounters leading up to one's choice of a partner do not lessen the work of marriage or make it any 'easier.' I'm convinced that the only thing that makes people have an easier time with marriage is 'choosing well' (which presumes that one has the tools to do so) – or 'lucking out' (meaning that you end up with actual husband material not by doing any deliberate homework of your own, but by pure chance).

Let's remain spiritual without over-spiritualizing matters in life – including the process of choosing our mates. After I made up my mind to file for divorce, I visited with a pastor who had known my former spouse and I as a younger couple. One of the things he said that day was that 'Marriage is more physical than spiritual.' Now, this pastor is one of the most spiritual men I know.

Wow, I thought. *Wish I'd known that years ago!*

We all know of some non-Christian or even non-religious couples who are really happy in their relationship with one another, with some of these happy marriages spanning decades. There's something to be learned from such couples, I think – something that goes beyond just avoiding the unequal yoke. Please note that I'm not recommending that anyone do anything unbiblical. I'm just saying that I think we can learn something useful from different models of success. They may not be 'Christian,' but they are doing something right – and we shouldn't be too proud to learn what we can from that.

If you regard yourself as a Christian believer, that's great. You know what the Word says: choose someone that shares your faith so you can go on doing what you do for the Lord unhindered, etc. But remember that you won't be floating on the clouds in the heavenlies together just because you're Christians. Christians and non-Christians alike need to take the time to raise their children, to take care of one another during periods of illness, to comfort one another when a parent dies, to pay the rent, to pick up the children from daycare or school ...

If the person you choose to marry is simply not a nice person, then their prayer warrior status, or ability to lead worship with anointing won't change the fact that they're not *nice*. So don't be distracted or overly-impressed by outward manifestations of spirituality. I know far too many Christians that simply are not nice people, so choose carefully. In marriage, a lot more time is spent tending to physical things than to spiritual things. It's just the way it is. You'll still spend most of your life at work after marriage whether you're a Christian or not – tending to physical things. If you're a stay-at-home mom, you'll still spend more time raising kids and keeping your household than praying. It's just the way it is. So choose your partner with that in mind, while not neglecting spiritual things, either.

I love something that Dr. Robin L. Smith says in her book *Lies at the Altar: The Truth about Great Marriages*.

She says: '*Values are what you live, not what you believe.*'

As a 'believer' myself, this observation is one of the biggest revelations I have had since I first read the book. You and I can sincerely believe in something without making any effort whatsoever to live it out. And so, if you're a church-goer like me, you may find yourself surrounded by 'believers' who cling to certain values that they are not necessarily living out. I may really believe it's wrong to steal, but that doesn't mean I'm not a thief. All the more reason to listen to God (i.e., listen to your heart, where God speaks within you) and to apply common sense

63

and every form of godly wisdom you can in making your choice.

The young lady also asked me whether I think I followed God's direction/wish/will for me concerning my selection of a life partner. I did see some red flags prior to marriage, which I ignored, presuming that Christianity would make them disappear. But, as I know now, Christianity is not synonymous with irresponsibility. Fire burns the Christian hand and the non-Christian hand alike. Can God ensure that fire doesn't burn us like He did for Shadrach, Meshach and Abednego? I'm sure He can … but I've noticed that He hasn't done this for anyone since that incident.

As a Christian with the benefit of hindsight, I believe that we are required to take responsibility for ourselves, drawing on the wisdom and other resources God has already given us. Let's not decide not to do our homework because we think God is our fall back plan, or because we think Christianity is our 'crutch.' Doing so usually results in our wallowing in bitterness and in our pulling away from God, convinced that He didn't do what He could to protect us. "*Do your homework,*" I said to this young lady. "Learn who you are, what you like and don't like, the sort of people you like and don't like, and the things that are important to you. Then, choose accordingly." Oftentimes, the problem isn't that we don't have the skills to choose well; the problem is that we make our choice before we have taken the time and effort to know ourselves well enough.

'[B]e changed within by a new way of thinking. Then *you* will be able to decide what God wants for you; *you* will know what is good and pleasing to him and what is perfect' (Romans 12:2, NCV. Emphasis added).

My wedding ring

We got a good deal on my wedding ring. It cost us $75 at Sam's Club, and that was a lot of money to us back then. It's a simple, gold wedding band. I forget how many karats.

I never dreamt about what my wedding ring would be like. Apart from the fact that I'm not big on jewelry (except for earrings!), the sort of ring I would wear just never seemed terribly important to me. What mattered to me was to have a solid marriage, no matter what kind of ring I wore.

When we got it, I remember thinking to myself, *I bet this will fade in a year or so.* Although $75 was nothing for us to sneeze at back then, I knew that there were much more expensive, sophisticated, beautiful rings. *If it ever fades in the years to come, we can always buy a better one,* I thought.

We bought matching rings at the same time, for the same price.

For twelve years, I had this habit of playing with my ring: pulling it off from its tight spot, where it had left a slight mark on my skin, and rotating it around and around my finger. I enjoyed doing that for some reason. Once in a while, I would pull it off completely for a split second – just to see if it was still possible

– and then quickly put it back on again, petrified of the idea of losing it.

It didn't cost a lot, but it meant a lot. It represented the hopes and dreams of two young people with their whole lives ahead of them. It was a symbol of our partnership, our covenant.

My husband, despite his propensity for misplacing things, kept his ring firmly in place without a problem for the first three years of marriage. By the end of the third year, his business ventures began to take him to another country. When he got back from one of his trips – either late that year, or early the next – he arrived without his wedding ring. He'd lost it, he explained, when I pointed it out.

How do you lose your wedding ring? I wondered.

But he bought another one soon enough for me to think nothing more about it.

When he returned from his next trip, he arrived yet again without his wedding ring.

"How do you lose your wedding ring?" I asked (out loud, this time).

"I miss you when I'm gone," he explained. "And so, when I go to bed, I take off my ring and put it on the pillow by my side. It makes me feel like you're there with me."

Weird, I thought.

But I bought it.

He purchased yet another ring. This one was bigger with a bold design. A bit too gaudy for my liking.

The next time he got back, his wedding ring finger was bare, as usual.

I never asked about his ring again.

I honestly don't know why.

Perhaps I had just resigned myself to the fact that my spouse was careless and lost things all the time. Perhaps I was just too weary taking care of a small child to want to bother with an adult. Perhaps I just stopped caring – about the rings, about the tedious relationship – long before I even realized it myself. Who knows?

I finally took my wedding ring off a little over a year before my divorce. As I considered the various events that had unfolded over time, wearing it just seemed like a farce. There was no longer a covenant to speak of, and so wearing a wedding ring no longer seemed to hold any purpose. I put it in my jewelry box, where my earrings and necklaces have kept it company ever since.

My wedding ring never faded. My $75 wedding ring from Sam's Club.

After 14 years, it remains intact and almost as good as new. When I open my jewelry box to look for a pair of earrings, it shines back at me, brilliantly, knowingly, mockingly, from its new home.

Despite its arrogance, I still keep it. I would say I treasure it, actually. I respect it. It has stood the test of time, and there's something to be said for longevity, consistency, and constancy.

It's not a competition, and there is no deadline

Some people I know seem to be under the erroneous impression that, since I *actually got a divorce* (something African, Christian women rarely ever do), I must possess 'special' qualities – some sort of mystical power, some sort of 'anointing,' almost (for lack of a better word) that can somehow be transferred to them if I would only say the word. If I would only cooperate and 'transfer' it to them, they could find the strength to finally make the same decision, get divorced, too, and live 'happily ever after.'

Personally, I do not fantasize about having anyone join me on this journey that divorce represents. I don't aspire to be the instrument that's used to extract women from their marriages, even though I know that some are really struggling with trying to make a final decision about their marriages (whether to stay or leave) – and almost see themselves as 'failures' when they don't get round to it.

I can really relate to how difficult it is to make a decision one way or another, and I wish everyone in this situation could have an easier time with it. But I have as much respect for those in intolerable marriage situations who feel they must stay as I do for those who feel they must leave. Neither decision is made lightly, and neither is easy. As I have said to some women in the past: this is not a competition. This isn't a game to see who gets divorced the fastest. This isn't a test to see who's got the most 'guts.' There is no deadline by which a decision must be made. And sometimes, making no decision at all for a while might actually be the best decision.

When women ask me if I think they should get divorced, I realize they're looking for someone to take the unwelcome burden of this very personal decision off their shoulders – and that they think I qualify for the job, having come to my own decision. When women ask me if I think they should get a divorce, I tell them as gently as I can (not wanting to hurt their feelings) that I never had to ask anybody if I should get divorced. And that if you have to ask someone else whether you need to get a divorce, then you absolutely should not get one.

How come?

Because even if you do find someone that's prepared to give you the answer you want to hear – even if another individual provides the answer that you're too terrified to give yourself – the hard work of sticking with (or leaving) a marriage, still remains yours … and yours alone.

I never give a 'yes' or 'no' answer to the question of whether or not to dissolve a marriage, no matter how much my soul might ache due to some women's marital situations. Because even if I really do think your marriage is a sham and should no longer be allowed to see the light of day … if you do walk away from it, I won't be there to share your financial burden. If you do walk away, I won't be there to hold you at night. If you do walk away, I can do nothing to ease your loneliness in the aftermath of divorce. If you do walk away, I won't be there as a companion you can talk to, confide in once in a while. If you do walk away, I won't be the one to have to raise your children alone ... the one to have to explain to your children why Daddy doesn't live here anymore.

Every woman has a unique set of marital circumstances, and there are millions of 'good' reasons why women stay, and millions of 'good' reasons why they leave. I have no special powers, and I'm certainly not Superwoman. My divorce decision was a consequence of my particular marriage situation. Even then, I did not arrive at it in a day, nor a month, nor a year.

I initiated an informal separation which lasted four years (after the first two, I had made up my mind without a shadow of doubt), simply to give myself time and space to think. During those years, I left no stone unturned in my mind, weighing my options, asking myself what a divorce would realistically mean for me, how it would change my children's lives, my life, and if I was really ready to handle it. From the questions I asked myself emerged the following startling responses:

Question: Could I really manage without a husband, as a single parent?

Answer: After the first three years of marriage, I spent the next decade as a single parent. Married, but alone the vast majority of the time. Our cross-country marriage meant that I had already learned to manage, then ignore, and finally, overcome the anguish of being a 'married' woman with a husband that was hardly ever present. Unintentionally, through his lengthy absences, my spouse taught me that I could do without him, and that I could also raise the children on my own.

Question: How would I manage financially on my own, with two children?

Answer: After the first five years of marriage, I sort of figured that, although married, I was pretty much on my own financially. With the unpredictability of business, I had learned by my fourth year of marriage that I needed to work (and work hard) if we were going to have a steady income. I was basically on my own, both physically and financially, since that year, and continued to be for the next decade. In a bid to be a 'help meet' for my husband, I made the mistake of most 'capable' women who haven't been advised against it and ended up meeting all the family's financial needs. Subsequent to the fourth year of marriage, I honestly don't recall asking my spouse for money for anything, really (big mistake!!). *After all*, I thought, *we're a team. My money is his money; his money is my money. What difference does it make whether I pay for my new hair-do, or he does – whether I pay the school fees, or he does?* As hard as it was to shoulder the responsibility of the family's finances, it prepared me with the knowledge and confidence that I could do it – because I'd been doing it for a decade already.

Question: What would I tell the children?

Answer: The children were as used to being without their Dad as I was, fortunately and unfortunately. So this wasn't a big leap for them by any means. And I was open with my eldest as soon as things fell apart (my youngest is still too young to really 'get' it), providing just enough information as was age-appropriate, and creating space for us to talk whenever he needed to. I have

71

told my children that their father *loves* them and that I fully release them to *love* him back.

Question: How would I deal with changes to my social life as a result of the divorce?

Answer: I *have* no social life. I'm one of those people who don't get out much. I'm a 'home-body' if there ever was one. **I love** being in my house! I have a few *really* good friends, most of whom live outside the country, so social concerns (whether within or outside the church) weren't (and still aren't) a big issue for me.

Question: What would I do if I got lonely?

Answer: I wasn't afraid of loneliness – but only because I'd been lonely most of my marriage and life still went on. I reminded myself that loneliness isn't caused, necessarily, by the absence of an individual. You can still feel terribly lonely with your spouse right beside you in bed. I had survived the loneliness of my marriage, and if the loneliness hadn't killed me while married, it wouldn't kill me while divorced. Loneliness had become so familiar to me that I didn't notice it anymore, except on the occasional weekend when things didn't get too busy. But my life was busier than ever, and I could find ways to fill those couple of hours of loneliness which didn't come around every single weekend, anyway.

My internal responses to these and many other questions were convincing enough to make me realize I had little or nothing to lose at the end of the day. I realized that a divorce would not change my life in any drastic fashion.

But these are *my* questions and *my* answers, based on *my* realities. They may have little applicability for the woman next to me.

And, again, this is why, when women ask me if I think they should get divorced, I have no answer to give. My situation is different from yours, and the only one that has the real answer to that question … is you.

The gift

L ike most men I know, my former husband loved cars and always seemed to be on the look-out for a reason to get a new one. I don't know much about cars myself, and I'm not picky about them as long as they're reliable. There were a number of occasions when he badly wanted a brand new car for whatever reason, and I didn't.

In one particular instance, we couldn't really afford a new car at the time and I didn't see what was wrong with our old one. He probably bugged me about the need for a new car for over a year. Each time, I patiently pointed out why it was a bad idea.

And then came my birthday.

He got home from work that evening and rang the doorbell. I opened the door and he pointed to his surprise birthday present for me, sitting out in the driveway: a gleaming, brand new car.

I was absolutely *horrified*.

I had a split second to make a decision about how to react. I was in a daze, and for a moment, everything seemed to be happening in slow motion. In front of me stood my husband, dangling a new set of car keys before my eyes and mouthing the words "Happy Birthday! Go ahead and take it for a test drive." His eyes and hesitant, artificial smile pleaded with me to act 'right.' To not embarrass him in public by looking unimpressed. Out of the corner of my eyes, I caught a glimpse of my Vietnamese neighbor, perched on his front porch, smoking his usual evening cigarette. He had a large, expectant grin on his face and an expectant light in his eyes, just waiting for my delighted reaction.

In that split second, I chose cowardice.

I got a hold of myself, plastered a wooden smile on my face (my neighbor was watching keenly, after all), reluctantly took the keys (with an 'I-can't-believe-you-did-this-I'll-kill-you-later' glance at my spouse) and walked stiffly toward my unwanted birthday present.

As I drove around the neighborhood for a minute or two, I was livid, confused, embarrassed.

How manipulative! I thought at first.

And then I chided myself for being unfair. *Most wives would be ecstatic to have a brand new car as a birthday present from their husbands. Why can't I just be grateful for the thought? Because we can't afford it, that's why! And because this isn't really for me; this is for* him. *But that's not fair – give the guy a break. Maybe he really meant well. Maybe his heart was really in the right place even if the decision wasn't the wisest. It's your birthday and you got a present. What's so wrong with that?*

I fought with these feelings until I pulled back into our driveway. As I stepped out of the brand new car, I resolved to be grateful.

My husband bought me a new car to show me how much he cares. That's all that matters for now, I told myself.

I look back on that decision made in a split second and I regret it. It was one of many decisions that I would change if I could go back in time. I tell myself that I shouldn't have participated in the charade for fear of what the neighbors would think and say. I should have confronted the feelings of embarrassment – mine and my former husband's – rather than merely burying mine and assuaging his. When I got into that car, instead of driving aimlessly around the neighborhood, I should've driven it straight back to the dealer. Although there would have been a short-term price to pay for this action, it would not have compared to the price we paid financially and emotionally in the long-run.

My birthday gift was repossessed a couple of years later.

Shoulda-woulda-coulda.

Nice girls finish last

Someone is on her way to visit me as I write this. She's not been married very long and is on her way to seek marital advice from – of all people – me. She has plenty of married, Christian people to choose from, so I should probably be flattered that she has chosen me. But I'm wondering if I really want to be drawn into these kinds of conversations. How useful can I really be here? I mean, it's not like if I'm 'useless,' but I would feel much more useful if I didn't have to do this covertly. I'm uncomfortable with the idea of giving marriage advice on the sly; with playing into this notion that seeking help in troubled married times is a sign of failure and therefore has to be done clandestinely; and with the idea that the issues can somehow be magically resolved through the efforts of one half of the couple alone.

I'm trying to get myself into the right frame of mind so I'll be prepared for her when she arrives. I'm telling myself that hardly anyone can get away with giving one part of an African couple marriage advice openly. It doesn't matter if you're a fellow married woman, a never-married woman, or a man, for that matter. No one wants to be the target of blame if things backfire. But when you're divorced, being in this situation has a unique feel to it.

What am I afraid of? I've asked myself.

I'm afraid that she's at her breaking point and she's looking for someone to give her permission to stop trying … and that she's desperately hoping that person will be *me*. I'm afraid of not doing justice to the situation – of being just like everyone else she probably approached before me; of addressing the surface symptoms of this troubled union and not getting down to the root problem – not because I don't know what the problem is, but because digging up the truth might prove to be too costly. I'm afraid of getting my hands dirty; of 'taking Panadol' for someone else's headache; of ending up caring too much; of doing a thankless job.

Ultimately, I'm afraid that I will look into her eyes … and see *me* from just a few years ago … and end up talking not to *her* as she is now, but talking to *me* as I was then.

To be on the safe side, I might as well let it all out now. Address this ghost so it can *get out of the way* and I can see this young woman clearly; see her for herself and honor her and her situation in their own right. Honor her in a way that I did not honor myself.

Based on previous communication, I understand that the troubled marital situation my impending visitor is itching to share with me is about many things. Many seemingly 'little' things that you repeatedly convince yourself you can live with because they're so *little* after all. It's about the myriad of little, unaddressed things that eventually construct a complex set of circumstances. And it's about the one or two 'big' things that may or may not spell the end, depending on how the two people involved in the relationship choose to handle things. I remember far too vividly what this is like.

To myself in my late twenties through to my mid-thirties, I would simply say: *Restrain yourself.*

Go easy on the 'over-niceness.' Redefine what niceness means. If 'niceness' leads you to become less 'like a woman' and more 'like a man,' then ... don't be nice. It just might save your marriage. As sincerely as you want to help, never, *ever* put yourself in the position of shouldering the family's entire financial burden. There is something about doing so (or about just giving money to a man) that gradually makes him less than a man. Well-intentioned as it may be, it has a castrating effect that may well be irreversible – at least where you are concerned. I'm convinced that even if a man apparently enjoys the convenience of having his woman 'bring home the bacon,' there's something within him that will simultaneously (and paradoxically) rebel and leave him trying to assert his manhood in other ways. Negative ways, more often than not. A man needs to be 'a man' with *someone*, even if he acts like he doesn't want to be one with you.

I remember receiving an email from my husband years ago when we'd been separated for about two years. He asked if I was finally ready to stop being a 'macho woman.' I was shocked that this was his assessment of me and I was equal parts mad and hurt that he would use this term.

'If I'm now a macho woman,' I retorted electronically, 'then you made me one.'

I can think about this dispassionately now, years later. I was piqued and hurt back then because I had spent years bending over backwards to 'help.' I was 'helping' because I was asked for 'help' directly and indirectly. I was asked time and again. I was 'helping' because I was programmed to 'help.' I was 'helping' because I couldn't just sit around and watch our lives and everything around us collapse.

Or couldn't I have?

What would have happened, I sometimes wonder, if I had just let the chips fall where they may? If I had just decided that salvaging the situation and figuring things out wasn't my job? If I had just been a tad less … *capable*? Or if I had at least just 'pretended' not to be?

But are mind games and manipulation and one-upmanship essential for a successful marriage? If they are, then our definition of 'success' is suspect. Why can't two adults just (as Dr. Robin L. Smith would say) 'show up and grow up'?

If I sound bitter, it's because … well … I sort of am sometimes. I wanted to win in this area of life. I was confident that I couldn't be anything but a winner here. And, lo and behold, I lost. *We* lost.

As for what I'm going to say to this lady today, I'm still blissfully clueless about that.

Help me, Lord. I need wisdom.

'Bitches' don't mow the lawn

This critical incident is clearly etched in my mind. My son was three at the time and one of his favorite toys was an annoyingly noisy toy lawn mower. We were in the front yard together and I was mowing the lawn with our black, electric lawn mower. As I hustled up and down the little hill that was our front yard, my son was right beside me, hustling right along with his bright red, *Fisher Price* lawn mower.

I had just started mowing the lawn that year and this was probably the second or third time. I was almost done and decided to take a break on the sidewalk, wondering if I was motivated enough to mow the backyard, too, or if I should hold off for another day. All of the sudden, I sensed I was being watched. An Asian neighbor – a grandma – was watching me with pitying eyes from her front porch across the street, and a younger White neighbor next door was watching too, with the same expression. The White lady's lawn was always immaculate – boy, did they know how to keep a garden going! It seemed to be her husband's favorite pastime. They both turned away one after the other when our eyes met.

I still remember the wave of embarrassment that engulfed me in that moment. I was terribly embarrassed by what I perceived to be their pity for me. I felt 'uncovered' and felt a sudden need to hide. I packed up the lawn mower, ignoring my son's protests, and scurried back inside.

The next day, I opened the front door to find the rest of my lawn had been mowed. The White lady must have said something to her husband because I caught a glimpse of him just finishing up my backyard.

I was *doubly* embarrassed.

The question is: Why was I mowing the lawn? Who sent me?

Well … my husband had started travelling the year before and was hardly ever around … so what was I supposed to do? Allow our house to be swallowed up by grass?

We were a young couple, just starting out; I was finishing up with school and only able to work part-time; he had ventured into business full-time. Money was tight – period. The lawn needed to be mowed and it never occurred to me not to do it. Maybe I should have asked a family friend's husband to help me out instead – but that wouldn't have occurred to me, either. Why disturb people when they have their own lawns to mow?

Now, I'm not against anyone mowing lawns if they want to, including women. I've been there, done that, worn the t-shirt. I know what it's like to want to help out because you truly consider yourself to be part of a team. It did not occur to me that taking on certain tasks was causing (it wasn't the whole cause, but I do believe it played a role) a fundamental shift in the relationship that would eventually prove to be detrimental. It would not have occurred to me to inconvenience myself in order to help 'keep my man in line.' Looking out the window at overgrown grass was a psychological inconvenience to me and I had to do something about it. To this day (in spite of my divorce) I cannot fathom inconveniencing my children and letting them get kicked out of school, for instance, when I have the money to cover the bill. That would go totally against my nature and it would literally kill me.

It's the 'Nice Girl' Syndrome.

And that's part of the problem.

I was frightened one day by something I heard Mark Gungor say on his TV program about Christian relationships, *Love, Marriage, and Stinking Thinking*. He basically said that if you took away the husbands of 'nice girls' and gave them 'good' husbands, the 'nice girls' would eventually sabotage these relationships with their 'niceness.' In the end, even the 'perfect' husband would begin to misbehave if you paired him up with a 'nice girl.' Because the 'nice girl' patterns would be repeated: catering to a man that hasn't proven himself, or that won't, or that has stopped doing so. Now that, to me, was scary. Makes you wonder, though: is it a bad thing to be a 'good' person? Ah-ah, what is it?

But I have to admit, when I look around me and pick out the few marriages I can see that are successful, *all* the wives share one common characteristic: they don't take any mess. Like my daughter, they ask for what they want, cause a ruckus if they don't get it ... and eventually seem to come out on top. They don't let anything slide. Every issue is confronted, no matter how it makes anyone else feel. And they don't feel 'bad' about doing it, either. Totally the opposite of 'nice girls,' who cringe at making anyone uncomfortable (except, of course, themselves).

This is all just perception and probably overly-simplistic, so I may be totally wrong, but that's the pattern I seem to have discerned. From Mark Gungor's perspective, all men are prone to 'misbehave' (forget about 'Christianity') and will do so if they know they can get away with it. And they know they can get away with it with 'nice girls.' This was a revelation to me.

After I got separated, a friend of mine asked me: "How could you do this to yourself? How could you allow this to happen?" She was referring to the fact that paying school fees and rent had become the norm for me. I was shocked by her indignation and filled with shame. Where was I when everyone else got this memo? How did I somehow grow up (in Nigeria, for that matter, for the most part) without 'knowing better'?

But, at the same time, what's up with some of these men? Shouldn't they want women with 'no *wahala*' and treat them right when they're privileged enough to win them? For whatever reason, only few men can handle 'niceness' well.

I just got an email an hour ago from someone I have worked with who's relocating elsewhere. Today is her last day at work in this country. Her message ended with the following words: 'Thanks for being such an organized and fabulously efficient, smart and lovely colleague, Nena!'

At first I read her message with a smile on my face. And then I read it again and the smile faded. The word 'efficient' gave me pause. I'm efficient, according to her. Fabulously so. I reconsidered the word with suspicion. After all, being an '*efiko*' got me to where I am now marriage-wise. But to be fair, it's also gotten me to where I am now, post-marriage; and frankly, it's not a bad place. It's a place that I have chosen. A place of peace and opportunities just waiting to happen.

In the end, I decided she was right. Yes, I am organized (at least to a certain degree!). Yes, I am efficient. Yes, I am smart. Yes, I am lovely. Maybe I just chose the wrong person to be 'nice' to (I'll forget Mark Gungor's theory for now), but it's not the end of the world. You live and you learn.

But what should a woman do (I've been asked a number of times) when the man fails to or is unable to shoulder his own share of the financial responsibilities in the home? Now that's the million dollar question.

I think the first thing, though, is to agree upon what his responsibilities are. Of course, hindsight is 20/20, and at 40, I know things now that I didn't at 26, when I got married. But don't let things remain in a state of flux. Be very clear in your own mind about what responsibilities each of you have. And then, based on my own set of lessons learned, I would simply say, if a man fails to live up to his responsibilities: *Don't stand for it.*

And there is no standard way of 'not standing for it.' Not standing for it will take different forms, depending on your personality and temperament. I didn't say 'Burn the house down,' but don't sanction it as being 'okay.' Because doing so is the biggest lie of all. It's *not* okay, and that's why your stomach churns even while you tell yourself it's 'okay.' And that's why things backfire – because anything based on a lie simply cannot flourish. Anything based on a lie is not sustainable. A woman's 'helping out' isn't meant to be a never-ending, ever-increasing exercise. Every woman will eventually come to resent it if she has to shoulder all the financial responsibilities in a marriage. Don't make the mistake of thinking that you can lie to yourself in order to sustain your marriage. Just tell the truth. The consequences will be less severe.

When you dishonor yourself, your circumstances conspire to dishonor you, too.

How I became a 'Nice Girl' (I think I finally get it … almost …)

I got an email message from a married, Christian woman that gave me food for thought. It was about my former 'lawn-mowing' ways.

"Mowing the lawn??" she asked. "Why ever? I will have to have found a few life-threatening snakes before I even dare; still, I'd hire someone to and fold the bill, waiting for the Hubby. I'm half Igbo, so 'the men must do the large part.'"

I don't know why I never asked myself 'Why ever?' Why that was not a response for me at all. For me, 'Why?' wasn't even a question that arose and I would love to get to the bottom of why it was not. Through my own marriage (and not to suggest that anyone else's is or will be like mine), I learned much too late that 'folding the bill waiting for the Hubby' helps ensure a man remains a 'man.' What I didn't suspect is that far too many men these days need this sort of 'help.'

The lady in question mentioned being half Igbo. Ironically, I'm 100% Igbo in that both of my parents belong to this Nigerian ethnic group; I spent a considerable amount of time in my village while growing up (like most Igbos do – or at least used to do); and even though I didn't really live in Igboland, I was surrounded by Igbos in the part of southeast Nigeria where I was raised. And yet, I remained totally oblivious to the useful cues that some Nigerian girls are really well-versed in.

A non-Nigerian family friend married to an Igbo lady once said to me: "But you're an Igbo woman. How did you allow this to happen? When my wife and I were dating and started talking marriage, she said to me, 'Look: Where I come from, men take care of women and not the other way round. I expect you to take care of me. My money is not your money.'"

I was terribly impressed. *What was wrong with me? Why couldn't I be like that?*

In my attempt to analyze this issue to death, I have thought a lot about my parents.

In some ways, my father was the most fascinating man. To lend further credence to my 'Igbo-ness,' he was what one might call the 'stereotypical' Igbo man: an *excellent* provider and care-taker in general, a problem-solver, peace-maker, and the unequivocal king of his castle. At the same time, he was what one female Nigerian scholar aptly referred to as 'the first male feminist' she ever met. He never hid his admiration for strong, ambitious, intelligent, independent women and was the biggest motivator, supporter, and cheerleader of women that clearly wanted more for themselves.

My mother worked, but not because she had to. I think she did so more because she was 'groomed' for it by her husband than anything else. After all, she never had to pay a single bill in her life. But then, perhaps that wasn't so unusual for her time. My sister's friend continually asserts that my mother is her 'hero' (much to our amusement!). From her perspective, my mother raised six kids and saw each of them go through college without spending a penny. In her words, "I want to know the secret!" In retrospect, maybe she has a point.

I want to know the secret, too – which is strange, considering that this is the woman that raised me.

When I really think about it, though, I suppose I *do* know what the 'secret' was. I know because I watched it in operation. The secret resided in marrying someone much older than you; someone that had already essentially 'made it' in life; someone who held off on getting married until he was sure he could (in stereotypical Igbo fashion) take care of you and everything else. The secret was in allowing choices to be made for you – even mundane ones – no matter what your opinion was (which was the case for my mother), rather than in having any real choices yourself.

When Fran Drescher got divorced, one of the things she pointed out (in her book, *Cancer Schmancer*) was how scary it felt to be on her own for the first time since the age of 15 or 16. She and her ex-husband had been together for practically her whole life. I was struck by the fact the she said she had never so much as bought a piece of furniture (not that furniture is a 'small' item) without asking, 'Honey, what do you think?' I could only imagine how difficult the transition from marriage to divorce must have been in this particular case. In my mother's case, she had never bought a piece of furniture, period. My father furnished all the houses we lived in – decided on the décor and bought it. Today,

I wonder whether perhaps a total lack of interest on my mother's part sometimes contributed to this dynamic. I'm not sure. But growing up, I perceived it as a total lack of *choice*.

Messages about her lack of choice around myriad issues were relayed and received directly, indirectly, and often. Growing up, I cringed at the more direct instances of this and subconsciously made a decision that the dynamics of my marriage would be different. I wasn't searching for an inordinate amount of responsibility, but I did want to feel like I *mattered*, to feel respected. Now, don't get me wrong: of course my mother mattered. But what I mean is, I wanted to decide what I wanted to study and study it. I wanted to decide which school to attend based on my own interests and my own research. I wanted to give input into where we would live or where the children would go to school. I wanted to have a chance to do many of the things that my mother didn't.

The secret is that there *is* no secret. My mother's marriage was a matter of circumstance, rather than a result of any intricately planned strategy or 'bitchiness' on her part. Many decisions were made for her because she got married practically as a child; and in the eyes of her husband, and in her own eyes even, she remained a child. I look back now and also realize that there were a good number of decisions that she didn't make simply because they didn't particularly matter to her. Why bother when your partner was an excellent decision-maker (and was able to finance his decisions)? And so perhaps what I perceived as lack of power as a child was sometimes, in actual fact, a mere lack of interest.

As much as I wanted to be a wife, I did not want to be treated like a child, and I was attracted to a man that would not treat me like one. One who wasn't much older than me. One who was just starting out in life. One who was on his way up and needed a partner to get there. And so maybe my so-called 'niceness' needed to feed on my partner's 'neediness' in order for me to have a sense of validation.

Ironically, it's almost as if my marital circumstances, coupled with my fears of being irrelevant, 'made' me into the sort of woman that I was convinced my father admired. But being treated like a 'man' in the end is something I hadn't bargained for.

Well ... at least I got what I wanted ... (sort of).

(☺)

The gift of discernment

I've learned that discernment is a gift. Like any other gift or present, it's meant to be acknowledged, opened up with excitement, examined, appreciated, and put to use.

I'm referring to discernment in the everyday sense of the term: 'the ability to pick up on details or have a good insight into something,' as someone defined it on WikiAnswers. 'The ability to recognize or distinguish the true nature of someone or something. Discernment and wisdom are close cousins. Personally, discernment means that I can "see through" (discern) a situation and decide whether that situation is good or bad, for instance. I use discretion with a person that I have discerned to be bad for me. I have deducted/discerned through watchful eyes, that not everything is what it seems.'

I struggled in the area of discernment for most of my Christian life. I can identify many different situations in my life where I escaped by the skin of my teeth, not because I discerned any danger, but just by the grace of God. I drifted through life, largely clueless about a lot of critical things happening around me – or under my very nose.

One good thing borne out of the demise of my marriage has been a heightened sense of discernment on my part. It has taken me nearly forty years to begin to 'get a clue.' Better late than never, I suppose.

I remember God trying to get my attention as a married woman quite early on. Around my second year of marriage, I had the same strange dream twice in the space of a few weeks. It was a really short dream – so short and to the point that I hesitate to even call it a 'dream.' But both times, it came while I was asleep, I would wake up right afterwards, remembering it vividly, and would lie in bed, trying to fathom what it was all about. Was it just an ordinary dream, or was there more to it?

In the dream, an old, shriveled, faceless man, with what looked like an old (maybe even tattered) shirt, appeared to me. For whatever reason, I could never see his face. It was always blocked out by the darkness, and so I could only see him from the neck down. Both times, he pointed his finger straight at me, and said with urgency in his voice: "*Pray against marital unfaithfulness.*"

The first time I had the dream, I prayed about it as I lay in bed early that morning. The next time I had the dream, I brought it to the attention of my prayer partner at the time. We spent time praying about it and against it, during one of our prayer times together. Around the same time, I also brought it to the attention of my spouse. He brushed it off, making a comment about my needing to address any hidden insecurities I might have, rather than give too much attention to a dream. This made sense to me … and so I brushed it off, too.

I never had the dream again.

As the years elapsed, I had a couple of reasons to at least suspect that infidelity was a possibility in my marriage, but I never did reach the actual point of suspicion. Again, I brushed it off – even on two occasions, much earlier on, when clear 'evidence' was staring me right in the face. I methodically re-defined the evidence, and decided that it wasn't proof of anything.

Was she in denial? I'm sure many must have wondered.

Actually, I wouldn't describe it as denial at all. I could not deny what I did not believe existed in the first place. I think the word *naïveté* provides a more apt description. I naïvely believed that only 'certain people' were susceptible to the temptation of infidelity, and that few of those people were Christian. I naïvely believed that even if one was tempted in this area, one would try to deal with it by communicating, getting counseling – whatever – not necessarily for my benefit, but because one held being in God's 'good books' as a high priority. And so, as far as I was concerned, infidelity was not something I needed to worry about, as one Christian married to another. Besides, there was so much for a Christian to lose by being careless in this area of life. Why bother? Your wife is sexually available to you, and you can have sex anytime you want. Honestly, how different was one vagina from another, really, that one would repeatedly feel the need to take this sort of a risk? Of course, I'm being overly-simplistic now by presuming that infidelity is always just about the sex and sexual organs, but come *on*.

The affair with a friend of mine finally laid my naïveté to rest. Two other friends experienced an instant unease the minute they met her, for reasons they could not explain. I now realize that they had their discernment antennae up, and could sense that something was not right, would not end up right. I was slightly put off by their attempts to warn me. They were both married, and I put it down to the paranoia of married women who engage in all kinds of 'gymnastics' to keep their husbands in line. One of my friends clearly said, "Pray about your relationship with this person. Each time I see her, I feel something negative in my spirit. I don't know what it is, but just pray about it." I honestly don't remember whether I did or not.

When it all came crashing down, I thought back to those moments and wondered how, in less than a minute, my friends were able to see what I couldn't see, sense what I never sensed. How come I didn't have what they had?

I have had a lot of time to reflect over my life, my marriage, and how I got here. As I look back now, I realize that I have always had discernment – I just didn't know what it was and how to pinpoint it. And because I didn't know what it was, I was unable to acknowledge it, treasure it, and use it. When I look back, I can identify those moments when I had a 'check' in my spirit. A fleeting sense that something is not 100% 'kosher.' It's often so fleeting and subtle that it can easily be missed, brushed off, or overlooked.

I can clearly look back now and remember how I could sense *something*, even though I couldn't quite put my finger on it. A 'check' in my spirit when he would call me at work, just to ask about something mundane, and I would innocently ask where he was, out of curiosity, and he would hesitate before responding. A sense of something being a bit 'odd' when he would explain that a chunk of money disappeared due to an emergency he supposedly had with the car. There wasn't much reason to doubt this explanation, but I remember having a strange feeling about the whole scenario. A sense that I wasn't being told the truth. I would brush it off. How ridiculous – why would my husband be anything but truthful to me? I can look back now and see the expression on his face. An expression I had seen so many times before, but only now recognize as being worn each time something was not quite right. I can look back now and actually pinpoint the exact times when things that should not have been happening were happening right under my nose.

Through my marital catastrophes, I finally found my sense of discernment. What a priceless gift!

These days, I treasure this gift like never before. I pay keen attention now to what is going on in my life, and I'm excited to see that when I sense something isn't 'right' – even if I can't explain it – I'm usually right. I used to think that as a Christian, it was my duty to embrace everybody right away, ignoring whatever misgivings I might have felt about certain individuals because the misgivings weren't based on anything tangible; they weren't based on anything but a nagging *feeling*. Not anymore.

I think the way in which discernment plays out is probably different for each of us. The key to figuring it out, though, is to pay attention – to yourself, to your instincts, to your spirit, to your impressions. To whatever you call it, as we all may have a different name for it. Personally, I have learned that my very *first* impression of a person (for instance) is critical. There have been many occasions on which I initially have a 'weird' feeling about someone I just met, but then, with the passage of time, that impression changes based on how the relationship grows, and we might even end up as good friends. This evolution in my feelings can then end up fooling me because it tends to make me forget what my very first impression was. And so, my strategy is not to lose sight of that first impression, no matter how well a relationship seems to be progressing. If it calls for my being careful in a particular relationship, then I don't brush the warning off. I keep it at the back of my mind and I am rarely surprised, later on, when really negative issues begin to crop up in the relationship concerned.

These days, I realize that God is speaking to me *all the time*. All I need to do is pay attention.

The help

I was in the kitchen that evening, standing at the sink, washing my hands, and just about to break my fast. It was February and my church dedicates this month annually to fasting and prayer in preparation for the year ahead.

It was then that they broke the news.

One started out, hesitantly, and the other two, looking equally uncomfortable, corroborated her story. They had not planned to tell me, they said. But when a close friend of mine paid me a visit a week after spending the night in my bed, and acted as if nothing had happened – and when they observed how oblivious I was – they decided they couldn't bear it any longer. They knew they were opening up a Pandora's Box, but were more scared of letting me live perpetually in ignorance.

It's hard for me to do relationships superficially, and so even though these three young ladies were the hired help in my home, over time, they each became my 'older daughters.' In the end, their loyalty towards me won out. Without them, I probably never would have found out that my husband was involved with my close friend. Without them, I probably never would have believed it, anyway.

They had all suspected it right from the beginning, and tried to draw my attention to it in subtle ways several times before, but I was always totally clueless as to what they were getting at. And then on this fateful day, they felt like they had to tell me directly. They were scared to death as they understood the possible repercussions – for my lovely, Christian family and for their employment. They were also convinced that no one would believe them. They were 'the help,' after all – invisible to many of the people they work for.

I have never doubted a word they said that day. Despite the shock and disbelief that this was not a dream I would wake up from – that this was actually my life playing out before me like a Nigerian movie – I believed them.

While the information they shared with me no doubt prompted my 'awakening' from a trance-like existence, it was certainly not the only incident in my married life that had the power to do this. It's not clear why this particular incident caused my rude awakening while the others did not. After all, it was not more 'shocking' than a couple of other occurrences from the past. My naïveté had not lessened with the passage of time, either, so what made this incident different? The main difference, I can see, is perhaps that this time, there were other pairs of eyes – three at that. It was almost as if I couldn't trust my own sight prior to this event. Or maybe I was just too afraid to. But this time, with witnesses, I could now 'see' with more clarity. Their account was later corroborated by other pieces of evidence – evidence that I could finally look out for by myself because I finally had my sight back.

I remember a number of things about that night and the couple of weeks following it. I remember how they had packed their bags in advance, assuming they were as good as unemployed, and yet still felt that breaking this news to me was more important than their livelihoods. I remember, too, how (when most people in my world initially assumed they had to be lying) they begged me to no avail for an opportunity to have my friend tell them to their faces (and in front of me) that she didn't spend that night at my place. In my bed. I remember believing them completely while still being absolutely incredulous – incredulous that this really can happen in real life to 'people like me.' Incredulous that this happened when I'd only been out of town for five days.

It took me a while to absorb this news completely – a long while. Even more than three years after this incident, the very notion was still a jolt to me.

I have been asked (including by my former spouse) how I can be so sure this wasn't just one big lie, deliberately designed to destroy my marriage. My sister says that, had she been in my shoes, she would have been very skeptical – not necessarily because of the involvement of 'the help,' but more because her trust level for an outsider would simply never be that high. As she put it: "Maybe [it's] because I am Nigerian and wired that way: everyone else is an 'enemy' of your progress; no one is as invested. You just don't tell someone that their husband is cheating – your own mother won't tell you, neither would your best friend. Not without some malice – at least, so we think." She ended by applauding what she referred to as our courage. Theirs, for revealing this to me in the first place, and mine, for taking the word of the help in this situation when I could have looked away.

She made a good point. I wonder if I would tell a sister or close friend of mine that their husband was having an affair. It's a tough decision to make, but I think that I would – if the situation called for it. In other words, I would consider the sister/friend involved carefully to determine if they were the sort of person that would want to be told. If not, I would keep mum about the infidelity, but convey messages about protecting one's health in this day and age.

I'm the sort of person that would want to know.

When people ask me how I can be so sure this all wasn't just one big lie, I tell them that there's no reason under the sun why these three girls would want to hurt me and my family in this way. Doing so would serve absolutely no purpose.

I am reminded of Naaman's wife, who was served by a young girl (I Kings 5: 1-2). Naaman, a valiant soldier and a great man by any account, was leprous. The young girl who served his wife had the key to his healing, not because she was a healer herself – but because she had information. Valuable information that she passed on to her mistress. Her mistress took this information seriously and her husband got healed as a result (I Kings 5: 14).

In my case, I'm not so sure I would have instantly believed the information I had received if it had come from anyone else at the time (except my own family members). These three frightened girls saved my life. Their courage in telling an inconvenient truth slapped me out of a dangerous slumber.

I will never forget.

I cry sometimes

I cry sometimes.

I'm not a big crier. I'm the sort of person that (if I could ever get organized enough) would rather schedule a time to have a good cry – would rather 'pencil it in.' Ordinarily, I cry so infrequently that if I'm going to bawl, I want to do it purposefully. I want to really respect and pay attention to my feelings in that moment, and to whatever it was that had the power to move me so.

Because I cry so sparingly, I think I see my tears as being almost precious. I would rather not cry for just anything or anybody. The fact that God treasures my tears, too – that they are precious and meaningful to Him, really touches me. Psalm 56: 8-9 (NLT) says the following about Him:

'You keep track of all my sorrows. You have collected all my tears in your bottle. You have recorded each one in your book. On the very day I call to you for help, my enemies will retreat. This I know: God is on my side.'

My tears matter to God, and I am blessed by that. He is close to the brokenhearted; He rescues those whose spirits are crushed (Psalm 34: 18, NLT).

I never really created the time to have a good cry when the last thread holding my marriage together snapped. Instead, I mostly cried in visceral, 30-second spurts now and then, experiencing my grief deeply, internally. On two occasions, however, I vividly recall breaking down in spite of myself for a 'real' cry. Both times in public, both times 'unplanned.' Both times in complete exhaustion and in reaction to the utter disbelief that my reality was even possible.

I confronted the reality of the end of my marriage with a roller-coaster range of confusing emotions. Disbelief, sadness, utter shock, bewilderment, amazement, horror ... but ultimately, I always came back to a vague sense of relief. Relief that I could finally let go of the madness that had been my life for most of the marriage, and at last begin to contemplate a sane existence. When I cried back then, therefore, I was not mourning the loss of an individual. I was mourning the loss of a once cherished dream; the loss of what could have been and what would now never be.

Nowadays, when my eyes well up with tears once in a while, I'm very cognizant of the object of my mourning. Surprisingly to me, this is not about my former partner. On the occasions when I do tear up, I mourn the death of my life as it once was, the death of a life that no longer is. I mourn the loss of my innocence.

Understanding the actual object of my mourning has been extremely helpful. There has been a death. It's normal to mourn a death, and I probably always will mourn for the woman that once was, and all she hoped and dreamed for. But I'm so thankful that her death has not taken away my desire to live.

Life is precious. Live well.

Running into the 'Strange Woman'

If you're a married survivor of infidelity and the marriage means anything to you at all, you immediately became obsessed with knowing the details of the affair(s) – and if the details are not made readily available to you (which would be the norm), your 'life's mission' becomes to unearth them yourself. You go through moments when you think you're going crazy – because your partner almost convinces you that you are, or because of the sudden change in your personality from a balanced individual to an obsessive human being.

Personally, I could not concentrate on my work for the first four months. How God managed to cover me during that period, I will never be able to fathom. With my workload, you simply can't get away with blanking out for a couple of days, not to mention a four-month period. During that time, I moved through my days in slow motion. My brain just seemed to be in a fog when it came to work. I would spend the first half of the day trying, struggling, *fighting* to maintain enough presence of mind to at least respond to emails. I was terribly unproductive. The remainder of the day would be divided between staring blankly at my computer screen with my mind far, far away, and Googling 'marriage,' 'Christian marriage,' 'Christian marriage and infidelity,' 'Christians and divorce,' 'When the Other Woman is your friend' – any permutation of words that came to mind and that I hoped would bring answers.

I understand that unfaithfulness is a really difficult issue for erring Christians to admit to. The implications of unfaithfulness are also far-reaching, and so it seems logical enough for the erring party to want to avoid causing any further damage – to want to just put it behind them and everyone else and face the future. I cannot emphasize enough, though, to anyone in this situation, that there is no real future without the truth. Withholding the truth does not spell the end for the marriage, necessarily – if the marriage in question is built on outward appearance only. Sure, it's possible to grin and bear it and limp along. But I'm talking about a *real* marriage – the kind worth fighting for; the kind we all hope for. In a real marriage – the kind worth fighting for – the truth can, will, and does set you free. The truth is more powerful than the pain. The truth is the starting point for healing.

I've run into one of the 'strange women' a few times since I found out. The first time, it was by appointment, and the other times, we just happened to bump into each other. The first time, she asked if she could meet with us both to have a discussion. Her sibling and another couple – close family friends of ours who stood with us all the way during this ordeal – were also invited. We met at a neutral place, a public hang-out spot in the neighborhood.

I arrived at the venue eagerly, exhausted by all the deceit and so ready to let them know it was tough, but I'd forgiven them, and I'd get through it. We sat directly across the table from each other on wooden benches in the garden. She talked for at least forty minutes, uninterrupted. I looked her in the eyes, but she wouldn't look back. Her eyes flitted everywhere as she talked – everywhere but toward me. I continued staring at her in consternation. *What was wrong with my friend? How had she changed so drastically? She was here to finally tell me the truth, wasn't she? Why was she avoiding my eyes – something she had never done in my history of knowing her?*

My mind tried to follow her long speech. She talked of all the respect she had for me and my family, about how she looked up to me and my husband, about how we were the model Christian couple, about how much she loved us ... I was getting lost. *Why didn't she just get to the point?* My gaze wandered from her shifting eyes down to her lips. I could no longer hear what she was saying – my mind was no longer following. I watched her lips moving, wondering what she was talking about. My eyes moved back up to her eyes, which still refused to meet mine. The sound of her voice switched back on. She was saying that she had been falsely accused, that this was all a malicious scheme to ruin our close friendship.

I was disappointed. I had left my house and come out here for *this*? She could have told me this on the phone. We didn't have to meet in person for this. *Why wouldn't she look at me?* I took deep breaths and silently chided myself for expecting too much, for expecting anything at all. When would I stop being so naïve? When would I ever grow up?

Our family friends moderated this difficult meeting with skill and maturity. I was grateful to have them involved, to have solid people in this land where I have no relatives. My husband was asked if he had anything to say about all this.

"Well," he began, shifting in his seat, "On behalf of my family, I just want to apologize to her for all the pain that she has suffered as a result of being falsely accused. This whole ordeal isn't fair to her."

WHAT??!! No, he *didn't*!

My ears tingled in disbelief. I honestly could *not* believe what I just heard. I immediately burst into tears in spite of myself. Someone handed me some tissue.

That was the first time I had cried since I found out.

I sat defenseless next to my husband and across from my friend of just a few weeks prior and simply cried my eyes out – tears, snot, gasps, shudders, and all. They both responded with silence, neither looking at me: my husband staring straight ahead of him, looking like an indifferent statue chiseled out of stone, and my friend avoiding my eyes, staring beyond me.

I felt naked, exposed, and ashamed, without a covering.

Well, this is just peachy, I thought to myself as I blew my nose. He often complained that I never wanted to allow myself to be vulnerable enough to cry. Now that I was crying, I hoped he was finally satisfied.

We finally dispersed after everyone else said a few words. We walked into the parking lot, a defeated mass of six. It had been a waste of time for us all. There were no winners.

I didn't come face to face with my friend until probably a couple of years later or more. I rushed into my office building that day, almost late for a meeting. I caught a glimpse of a figure standing awkwardly in the parking lot as I rushed past, and glanced behind me briefly, feeling like I was being watched. Not noticing anyone in my haste, I entered the building and waited impatiently for the elevator by the reception desk.

A figure suddenly approached me. Hesitantly, shyly. I looked up and recognized the figure as the person I had seen standing in the parking lot, but hadn't recognized. As I finally realized who it was, she greeted me nervously. I greeted her back, not bothering to hide my surprise. I asked politely how she was, as the elevator opened up. She was fine she said, as I entered the elevator. As the elevator doors began to close, she suddenly stepped forward courageously and asked if I could please call her sometime. She had been trying to reach me on my phone for quite a while, but I simply never answered it and she eventually gave up.

"Please call me," she pleaded urgently. "Do you still have my number? I lost my phone, so I don't have your number anymore."

"I don't have yours anymore, either, but I know how to get it. I'm not sure if I'll call, but I promise to think about it."

The elevator doors closed. I caught a glimpse of myself in the mirror along the elevator wall as I reeled over what had just occurred. I was glad I wasn't looking bad.

Don't be silly, I said to myself. This wasn't a competition. It never had been.

She was looking good, too. Thinner, and a teeny bit different in a few other subtle ways, but still essentially the same.

I debated for about a week over whether to bother calling her or not. *Call her for what?* There was nothing to talk about. But the temptation was strong. She had pleaded with me to call her. Maybe she was finally ready to tell the truth. Although my husband wasn't ready to break down yet, maybe she was. Maybe she was as tired of it all as I was.

And so I called. In a nutshell, the phone call was a disappointment. I didn't get what I wanted. Rather, I got an abridged version of what I had gotten at the public hang-out spot a few years prior. And so, I hung up, finally accepting that it was time to move on. I had to learn that I would probably never get what I wanted (what I felt I *needed*) and that this was okay.

Not long after that, I bumped into her in the parking lot of my office building again. She had a doctor's appointment at one of the clinics in the building. Unlike the last time, when I didn't have even a split second to think about how to react, this time, I saw her approaching and I thought about it. I decided not to carry on with the charade, pretending like nothing ever happened. She came toward me with hope and eagerness in her eyes, a greeting forming on her lips. I averted my eyes haughtily and openly shunned her. She immediately got the message and swerved into a different elevator.

There! I said to myself, feeling victorious as I got to my floor and headed to my office.

The feeling didn't last more than a few seconds. I was overwhelmed by conviction as soon as I sat at my desk.

There, what? I asked myself.

What had I achieved? There were no victories here, no winners.

I got back up almost the very minute I sat down and marched back to the elevator. I knew which floor she was headed to. I got there and found her standing at the reception desk. I walked up behind her with a message from my heart on my lips. *Look, I was about to say, I'm hurt and I don't understand, but I don't hate you. It's hard for me to know what to say to you given all that's happened, but I don't hate you.* She turned around just as I reached the desk and immediately began narrating the predicament she was having with her appointment, almost as if she was expecting me.

"I'm sorry to hear that," I replied. "How are you doing? How have you been?"

"I've been fine. Things haven't been easy, but I'm fine. I was fired from my job and I'm about to move. I had an accident and broke my leg. Remember my car? It was totaled during the accident – here are the pictures. I'm being kicked out of my house. Auctioneers came by and threw all my stuff out. It's been really rough."

"Oh ..." I was speechless.

I stared at her, taking in the single crutch she was leaning on. I stared at her, thinking of the friend I had once known so well. All the responsibilities she had in her family, and how giving she had always been toward them. How much we had shared and how close she had been to me. How on earth was she going to manage in this city without a job? How could things have gone downhill so fast?

There was no room for gloating here. No winners, no victories. None of us had come out of this wreck unscathed. This had been an all-around tragedy for every one of us.

"I'm sorry," I said simply and sincerely.

There wasn't much more to say. This time, she had looked into my eyes, and if she still knew me at all, she knew what I was trying to say, what I was trying to do.

I went back to my floor, to my desk, and sat down with a sigh. The important thing was to be able to live with myself, and this I could now do comfortably.

What it means to be held

I love Natalie Grant's song, *Held*. I was drawn to this song by this Christian artiste ever before I knew any of the lyrics. I bought the CD a few years ago because of the haunting tune of *Held* in particular and finally listened to it carefully in my car one day.

The song is about situations in the Christian life that are difficult to explain away, and difficult to walk through. Like the mother whose innocent, two-month old infant dies, without a 'sudden healing' experience, despite her fervent prayers. We weren't promised a problem-free rose garden, but we were promised that we would be held through it all.

I love the way the song makes us confront the fact that sometimes, the miracle we want may not be the miracle we get – but that what we do end up with is no less of a miracle. I love the honesty of the words. Its core message is that, inasmuch as every Christian wants and expects a tidy, hassle-free, name-it-and-claim-it life, the truth is that not everything in our lives unfolds quite so tidily. And we don't always have the answers as to why.

When we find ourselves in an 'untidy' place in life, we want to know *why*. We're Christians, after all. *Why should we have to go through this?* we wonder. At that point, we can choose to feel short-changed and allow bitterness to seep into our souls ... or ... we can choose to be held.

We can choose to let Him hold us and allow His embrace to be enough. Allow all our vexing, unanswered questions to pale in comparison to the knowledge that He is with us and has a good plan for us.

We can choose to understand that our survival of a horrific situation is a miracle in itself. Sometimes, our very survival is the overlooked miracle – the one that's right under our nose; the one we usually do not recognize.

If I have to choose between getting all the answers to my 'whys' and the satisfaction of just being held without a word, knowing that everything will be all right ... I think I'll go for being held.

There is such comfort to be found in a meaningful embrace. With divorce, though, this is something that one must be prepared to live without – at least for a while. And sometimes, depending on the dynamics of a marriage, one must be prepared to live 'unheld' in marriage, too. I am convinced that God understands this need for human touch (having created it in the first place), and I am glad.

'The eternal God is your refuge, and his everlasting arms are under you' (Deuteronomy 33: 27, NLT).

I should be glad of another death

I just finished reading Chinua Achebe's *No Longer at Ease* a few minutes ago. All I can say is: *My goodness*. It's amazing what you miss when you're younger. I read it for the first time when I was probably 13 or 14. At the time, all I was interested in was the complicated, tragic romance between Obi and Clara (which, back then, I felt Achebe didn't spend enough time on). All these years later, I now see and deeply appreciate all the subtleties I had missed as a teenager. I am tempted to say that, in many ways, this book beats *Things Fall Apart* hands down, but I won't actually utter these words because that would be sacrilegious. I suppose one is just much easier for a person of my generation to relate to than the other and that makes it more poignant.

I read two-thirds of the book at first, and then paused for a day. It just got too excruciating. It was much too painful to watch the idealistic Obi gradually get swallowed up by his own humanity, by circumstances, by his country. I 'get' him, and I hurt for him.

I should mention that (shock and horror) I took three days off from work and tonight is my last night as a 'carefree' woman until December when (hopefully) I can have a real vacation. These three days away from the office were long overdue. As I constructed my automated 'out-of-office' message, it occurred to me that this was the first time I had ever done so. It's been almost a decade since I really just put work completely aside and let myself forget about it. Well, to be honest, I still checked my email regularly during this brief hiatus, but barely replied any messages. I felt really smug as I watched messages land in my inbox – smug about the fact that my automated message would let everyone know that whatever it was would have to wait.

Thank you for your message. I am away from the office until October 10th. I will respond to your message upon my return.

In other words: *Let the chips fall where they may. I'll pick them all up when I get back.*

It's been good for the soul, this brief respite. I have truly savored this time. I mainly hung around the house and did nothing much except serve as a short order cook for my children, whipping up whatever they asked for. And I spent time staring out of the sliding doors from my bedroom. I marveled at all the lilac petals that had accumulated on the balcony outside my room. I hadn't realized what a beautiful tree I had leaning against my balcony. I recall my mother finding the tree really irritating, given all the leaves it left on my verandah each day when she was visiting. She kept threatening to cut it down and I barely paid any attention.

I spent some time on my balcony, staring shamelessly into the neighbors' garden in the next compound. I'd never noticed what a lush garden they had. And I spent some time on my treadmill, delighted by the beautiful sunshine that streamed through the sliding doors. I noticed a beautiful little black, orange-breasted bird, with a bright orange beak, before it noticed me and flew away. I spent a couple of hours with my dear friend right around the corner.

When I was done reading the last page of *No Longer at Ease*, I went back to the very beginning to take one more look at the part of the T. S. Eliot poem that inspired the title:

We returned to our places, these Kingdoms,
But no longer at ease here, in the old dispensation,
With an alien people clutching their gods.
I should be glad of another death.

The reference to 'the old dispensation' brought to mind some malaise of my own which I experienced during my short period of much-needed rest.

I had not heard from my children's father in ages. I had mixed feelings about this extended silence. On the one hand, I was relieved about it because my impression has been that not hearing from him makes my life less complicated. On the other hand, I worried that our children would get too used to this, and that's probably not such a good thing. It's actually my children that make this silence an issue for me at all. It worries me that they've gone for months without asking to speak to their father, and don't seem interested in doing so even when I urge them to.

But over the last few days, I suddenly received a series of text messages from him out of the blue. I suppose I should call them 'rhetorical' text messages because I do not reply to them when this happens and I think he already knows that I won't.

First Text: A rather nostalgic message, reminiscing about the love he once felt for me (and the challenges of moving on as a result), affirming that marriage to me was no mistake, thanking me for the relationship that once was, and assuring himself (more than me) that all would be well despite the circumstances.

I wondered where this was coming from exactly. I noted with relief that the word 'loved' was in the past tense. Maybe he was just having a tough day. We all have them. Divorce is tough. Perhaps it's uniquely tough for African men. In discussing this with author Ekene Onu, she pointed out that most African men are not socialized to believe or expect that their wives ever can or will leave, and this has got to make divorce (when initiated by a wife) harder for them. I think it dawns on my former husband sometimes just how much he has lost, and that's got to be hard. His occasional messages to me out of the blue are plausibly a form of therapy for him, given that there is little room for such care in the typical, constricted, African male world.

He did mention a couple of years ago that he'd met someone and it was serious. They were talking marriage. I told him I was happy for him and honestly wished him every happiness. Maybe it didn't work out. Or maybe it did, but maybe he's just realized that she's just not 'me.' And maybe that's the hard part – trying to get really comfortable with someone else. I sympathize. But not to the extent of wanting to try and be my ex-husband's therapist.

Second Text (couple days later, 6:14 a.m.): A confusing text about the frequent dreams he's been having about me lately. In each dream, I am distraught and weeping. I ask him for explanations in these dreams.

This text woke me up from sleep and it took me a while to understand it. I then realized that he considered my statements in his dreams as sort of telepathic messages from me.

Lord, have mercy; I'm trying to sleep here.

Third Text (6:26 a.m.): More about my deep sadness. I cry throughout these dreams and feel misunderstood by him. He assures me that he understands and that he will make things right.

Sigh

This is why I don't reply. I don't get it and I don't want to – and I don't want to inadvertently encourage what I don't understand. I don't know how else to state the obvious without being rude: that ship has totally sailed.

Maybe he has this idea that if he holds out long enough, I'll eventually change my mind. This in itself shows a complete underestimation of the gravity of the situation. The 'old dispensation,' so to speak, makes me terribly uneasy. Without meaning to be too dramatic, I honestly think I'd rather die than return there. I just want to be left alone.

Hapu m aka, biko. *

(*Translation from Igbo: *Leave me alone, please.*)

The Dark Cloud

I stumbled on a Huffington Post divorce page feature: tweets from the public in response to the following subject: *The moment I knew: Readers share their divorce stories*. I read all 74 tweets that were selected for display. I could relate to several of them. Many were extremely sad, some were matter-of-fact, and others were actually sort of comical (not that there's anything really funny about divorce).

I gave a go at responding to it myself. At what moment did I know the marriage was over?

Really hard to say. I found that I couldn't answer the question in a succinct way. *It wasn't just one moment*, I thought to myself.

One person's tweet captured my own experience perfectly: "Was not just one moment. It was a thousand little disappointments and heartbreaks. Add them up over time."

Like all married couples, we had our issues. We were not the perfect couple (is there any such thing?), though we may have looked that way to some. A few issues we tried to deal with head-on, while others were swept under the carpet. But even then, there was this determination that no matter what challenges we faced, we were going to be together. The 'D' word was not part of our vocabulary.

We had both been on 'auto-pilot' for years. I would actually venture to say that we were on auto-pilot practically from the beginning of the marriage.

During our pre-marital counseling classes, our pastor at the time asked us to share one major thing about each other that caused us individual anxiety. I'm not sure if he was just being polite, but in his view, my soon-to-be husband had nothing to worry about. I, on the other hand, brought up the fact that sometimes, he would unceremoniously go into a state in which I couldn't 'reach' him. He would shut down for no apparent reason, either over something that I wasn't aware of, or over something that was really trivial, in my opinion.

I didn't use the term 'moodiness' back then because I just didn't know how to describe it. All I knew was that he would completely shut down, close off, and shut me out. The only way I could describe it for years (including to the pastor that day) was that it was as if a Dark Cloud would suddenly descend over him, and it would take the whole day (or a few days) for The Cloud to lift. And when The Dark Cloud was gone, there was no tangible explanation for why it appeared in the first place. It would leave me utterly confused. It was deeply painful for a person with my psychological make-up. I'm open, expressive, and I love out loud. When I feel low, I turn toward the people I love (including family and friends) rather than away from them.

He was pretty upset that I brought up The Dark Cloud with the pastor, which baffled me, since the whole point of pre-marital counseling classes is to iron out these things. Well, at least that's what I used to think. Of course these classes provide an opportunity for couples to learn what to anticipate in marriage and how to start working together to address the inevitable challenges. But I once thought that the purpose of pre-marital counseling was to help unearth buried red flags, and to then work the most problematic issues out before marriage. Plus, like many other women, I also viewed the classes as just one more thing to you had to do before you could get married in church. In my mind, once you got to this stage, the wedding was certain, and so it was all about 'fulfilling all righteousness.'

I now think these classes serve an even better purpose: They provide an opportunity to change your mind about marrying your fiancé when it becomes clear that the red flags are too red.

It was at that point – the point at which I realized we couldn't talk or be counseled about The Dark Cloud and several other issues – that I should have put on my Nikes and gone on a cross-country run without looking back.

But I didn't.

After all, wasn't I the one who, at age 21, looked straight into the video camera during my older sister's wedding, in my pretty lilac bridesmaid's dress, and gave her the following sagacious words of advice: "Just remember that love means making yourself of no reputation"?

And so I resolved to become an expert at making myself 'of no reputation,' like Jesus did (Philippians 2: 7, NKJV). That was my foolproof plan. And in my attempt to do so, few issues troubling the marriage were confronted head-on. I spent my time playing dodge ball – dodging issues and confrontation. It just seemed easier that way.

A few times (very few times) when I did put my foot down about something, things worked out okay.

For the most part, though, it resulted in visits from The Dark Cloud. These unwelcome visits could last for days – or weeks. The first visit was the day after we got married. Literally the next morning. It was such a stark contrast to his mood the day before, when he was clearly on a 'high.' I was filled with foreboding when I observed his crash from that height the very next day, but I comforted myself with the thought that he was probably just experiencing an anti-climax, which probably wasn't unusual. It was probably similar to the 'Graduation Blues,' I thought. You work so hard to graduate and when graduation day arrives, you wonder why you're not more ecstatic.

The longest visit by The Dark Cloud lasted three weeks, during which he didn't utter a *single* word. To say that I was confused is a huge understatement. In my mind, I replayed the scene that led to The Dark Cloud's visit over and over again, dissecting it, and going over it with a fine-toothed comb, trying to figure out if *I* was going crazy or if *he* was. All I could remember was that we were visiting my in-laws and I wanted to buy a particular gift for them. They made me feel so welcome the first time I visited and sent me home with gifts, including a humungous turkey (which I was too afraid to carry back by myself, since I never did learn how to carry a live bird). The yam season was long over and so I thought it would be nice to surprise them with a nice stack of rare yams. For whatever reason, my husband thought this was a bad idea, and in the process of my trying to get him to explain why, he took offense. That was it. Not a single word for almost a month.

It was sort of like the weather nowadays. Totally unpredictable (which is why a tiny umbrella is a permanent fixture in my handbag these days), and seemingly uncontrollable. And once the rains start, there is no telling how severe they will be or how long they will last.

Things got easier in this regard three years into marriage when he began to travel. As hard as it was to be on my own as a young married woman, it was also a relief not to have to live life walking on eggshells each day, never knowing for sure when the unwelcome visitor would be back.

To return to my initial point, I don't think there was a particular 'moment' or critical incident that let me know it was over. Rather, there was an accumulation of many little moments. In the midst of our marriage-on-auto-pilot, though, I do remember when I sensed something 'different' in the relationship. The year before the relationship gave up the ghost, I noticed a certain change in him. It was a very subtle change. No matter what, he was always the type of person to celebrate me, and to celebrate with me. He wanted big things for himself and for me, too. If I felt a bit down about something I wanted to accomplish but didn't attain, he always had an encouraging word. When I achieved something at work or church or anywhere else, he was always genuinely glad. I'm an introverted and naturally unambitious person who loves to live in her safe cocoon, while he's Mr. Ambition and Mr. Adventure. And so he would actually try to push me beyond my limits and get me to try new things and to press harder toward living up to my potential. And since I love conversation, I would tell him everything that was going on at work. And he would respond with genuine interest.

But that year, I noticed for the first time *ever* that whenever I shared an accomplishment with him (all excited, too, because I rarely got to see him), he would listen with an expression of extreme impatience in his eyes. Eventually, he started cutting me off and changing the subject. This was *most* unusual. I wasn't sure what was wrong, but I assumed that his years of trying to attain certain goals of his own to no avail were taking their toll. I could see how frustrating it had to be for someone like him – who generally moved with the speed of lightening – to have to wait for years, trying to realize his dreams. I rationalized that my 'little' successes in one or two areas were probably a painful reminder of what he had not yet achieved. I took 'my' successes and 'his' successes as 'our' successes – we both did for the longest time. But at some point that began to change. And so when I noticed this, I began to censor myself.

I was supposed to be a pro at making myself 'of no reputation,' right? And so I began giving Oscar-worthy performances, playing my role to the hilt. I began to erase my own news, to keep mum, to diminish myself, to make myself *less* … hoping it would make him feel like more. I didn't want my husband feeling uncomfortable around his wife, so I did whatever I could.

Little did I guess that this could never be a real, lasting solution. Whatever internal issues he was grappling with had to be confronted and dealt with by him. My trying to 'change' myself to make him feel better, while well-intentioned, was really a waste of both of our time. It made me live a lie and contributed to hampering his own quest for truth.

Plus, it did absolutely nothing to help get rid of that very unwelcome guest.

Mommie (in-law) Dearest

It's no secret that I'm in love with my mother-in-law. I suppose I should call her my 'former mother-in-law,' but that would be too much of a mouthful; plus, I still see her as 'current,' as present in my life, even though, technically, she's not.

At least I did something right, I say to myself when I think of her. I may have goofed in choosing the man to spend the rest of my life with, but I sure chose the right family to marry into. We got along with each other swimmingly right from the start, my mother-in-law and I. But then, everyone gets along with her. It's impossible not to as she has a heart of pure, Christian gold.

I visited her for the first time about a month before she became my mother-in-law. She pointed to a live goat in her backyard and explained it would be slaughtered for my meal. She had gotten it specially for me and later prepared the scrumptious meal herself. I was so touched. It was definitely love at first sight.

After marriage, our trips to Nigeria were spent exclusively in the village with her. Some of my friends were horrified at the idea of my taking the time to travel, only to spend my entire vacation in a remote village. I didn't miss city life, frankly. It would take me an average of two days to settle in to 'village life,' after which I would begin to relax and thoroughly enjoy the slow-paced, stress-free, mostly idle days in the village. She and I would have incessant conversations all day long. There was always something to talk about, to laugh about.

It's hard for me to describe the depth of our relationship. I know we're supposed to hate our mothers-in-law, and to 'pray that the mother of whoever we marry is already dead,' according to my sister's friend, but I really do love mine. I treasure the relationship we have (or had). A non-literate woman, she is one of the wisest, most intelligent, discerning, selfless, and caring people I know.

In the first few months after the divorce, I made repeated phone calls to a brother-in-law. Just to say hello to her. I could usually only reach my mother-in-law by calling his phone. He also used to be the in-law that called me the most. Each time, he very politely gave me some really good reason why she couldn't come to the phone. It took me a while, but I eventually got the message. I could understand his decision. She's in her eighties now and he is probably afraid that a conversation with me – the woman that left her son, that left her family – may not be too good for her health.

In thinking about this now, it occurs to me that the silence from my former husband's family in general has been deafening since last year when I made it clear at a family meeting that the relationship was over and the divorce papers had been filed.

How come I can't 'return' my husband and just keep his mother? I would sometimes wonder in all seriousness. *Who says they have to come as a package deal?* Society says.

You've left the woman's son and caused eternal embarrassment for the family members (members of a family with a strong Christian reputation), who will always have to try and explain what happened to their brother's 'Christian' marriage. Don't you think it's time you left the family – left your 'former' mother-in-law – alone?

My mother-in-law has always been deathly afraid of heights. For this reason, even though she has had many opportunities, she has categorically refused to get on a plane in order to visit one of her children who has lived outside the country for decades. She always said she would have to be sedated in order for this to ever happen. I was a bit hurt when I learned from a friend of mine (who ran into her) that she finally did make it onto an airplane and out of the country, sometime after the divorce. She was escorted on her trip by my former husband.

Why didn't anyone tell me about this historic moment? Why didn't <u>he</u> tell me? They can't pretend not to know what she means to me.

Well … I suppose I no longer have the right to know.

I do like to be fair, so I guess I can live with that. With the fact that, in getting divorced, I essentially gave up certain entitlements – including the entitlement of continuing to be seen as one of her 'wives,' as she refers to all her daughters-in-law.

If she's okay with the way things are, then I can live with that. But my worry is that she may think I simply no longer want to contact her. She may think I walked away without looking back, not realizing that I actually looked back (at her) many, many times before making my decision. And that I still look back (at her) even after the divorce.

How is it that in the quest to find the love of your life, you end up, instead, in a forbidden love affair with his mother?

At least I did something right.

Hide 'n' Seek

It took me about a month before I knew it was time for an informal separation from my spouse. A series of emails made the decision for me.

I fell into a fitful sleep one night – not long after the first time I met with one of the other women. As I drifted off, an idea suddenly came to mind. It suddenly occurred to me to head out to work earlier than usual the next morning and sift through my husband's emails.

I hadn't known his email account password for years. After the first two years of marriage, he became uncomfortable with my having this much information, and so he changed it. I recall my asking for it one day, wanting to check for something in his account. He hesitated, saying he'd changed it so many times that he had to be seated at an actual computer to remember what it was. I understood, having several passwords myself for everything from email accounts to bank accounts to health insurance accounts – several of which insist on a different configuration of letters and numbers for a password.

But one day, his travels took him to a remote area without internet access. He urgently needed to know if a particular email message had come in yet, and called me at work, in a different country, asking me to check.

"What's your password?" I asked. He gave it to me and I checked for him. I never thought about his password or email account again.

Until now.

I suddenly realized that I had filed his password away in my memory and could still remember it after all those years. I got up the next morning on a mission. I was in my office by about 6:30 a.m. and logged onto my computer, finding that his password hadn't changed.

Where do I even begin? I wondered, staring at the email account which had been established probably the very year after we got married. A certain name came to me for no particular reason at all. This person was the *least* likely, actually, in my mind, to have anything 'unusual' to communicate with my husband about. Still, I obeyed the prompting and sifted through all the communication I could find between them. I took my sweet time – about two hours – sifting through his email messages.

My hands began trembling as I read email messages spanning a few years, piecing together a portrait that I knew I didn't really want to look at. *Get a hold of yourself,* I told myself. I began to shiver as if I had a fever. *Get a hold of yourself. Hang on. You have to know for sure.*

Two hours later, I had had my fill. I called up my usual cab driver.

"Please take me straight to the bank," I said.

He looked at me curiously and with concern. "Okay," he said. "You came in really early today. Are you feeling well?"

I barely replied.

I clenched my fists, trying to stop the shivering, trying to breathe and calm down. On our way to the bank, I replayed the emails over and over again in my mind. I was fixated on the endearments and other signs of intimacy shared between them.

Who *was* this person? He never used endearments with me, and his email messages tended to be to the point and business-like most of the time. After some years, I resigned myself to the fact that this was just who he was. We all weren't born with a romantic streak, after all. So who was this stranger who suddenly knew the 'right things' to say to a woman? I breathed harder. He never sent me money, either. How could this be happening? Was this really happening?

'Honey … There are days I wish you were here …' she had written. Her emails almost always ended with 'I miss you,' written in a slightly coded manner.

How was this possible? I wondered. I had met this person once. A sort of business partner of my spouse, she had done us a favor at the time. She actually picked me and my son up at the airport (at his request) and later saw us off again, handing me a parting gift – a lovely piece of *adire* material. She had been so nice and helpful.

I resisted the urge to throw up. I breathed harder.

131

At the bank, my bank manager rushed out as soon as she saw me through the dividing glass.

"What's wrong – are you okay?" she asked, ushering me into her private room. "You look like death. You look so stressed. Here, have a seat."

I sat down, still trembling, and gave her a summary of what I'd just discovered. She gave a small, wry laugh. This wasn't unusual, she explained. It *wasn't*? I wondered, my head spinning.

"I used to feel sorry for you each time you'd come with him to the bank and apply for another loan. I wanted to ask you why you always turned it all over to him – why you never took any for yourself," she continued.

You did? I said to myself.

Fortunately, in the midst of all this, I was somehow filled with a remarkable level of lucidity. I instructed her to pay off my bank loans, transfer practically all of the remaining funds out of the country, and close down the account with immediate effect. She got down to business and gave me the paperwork, making things as easy as possible for me.

It seems strange, but the emails I discovered seemed like an even bigger blow than finding out my close friend slept in my bed. The thought that my spouse could be someone I wanted him to be with someone else, but not with me, was just too much for me to wrap my mind around. It all made no sense.

I marveled at the frailty of human beings.

A Beautiful Mind

There's a reason why I'm still not on FaceBook.

Okay – there are three reasons. All are based on either fear or puzzlement. Firstly, I'm not sure if I need (or can cope with) yet another distraction as a person who can barely keep up with (work-related) email. Secondly, although my younger sister has patiently tried to 'break it down' for me several times, I still don't quite grasp why people who *really* want to connect with me (or just want to see my pictures) can't simply email me (When did all this change and where was I?). Thirdly, and most importantly, as my sister dissected the rationale behind social media for me, I was suddenly filled with apprehension. I was newly separated at the time – not even divorced – and I wasn't sure that 'introducing' myself to the world and catching up with long-lost friends was such a good idea.

My sisters eventually gave up on trying to get me to 'join the 21st century,' but still filled me in on the exciting discoveries they regularly made via FB: a connection with a beloved third grade teacher after decades; weddings and births; news about the 'underdog' from high school who ended up making it big ....

As I was soon to discover, though, I was right: FaceBook probably wasn't such a good idea for me at that time in my life, and my personal abstinence from this tool wasn't enough to shield me from what was to come.

A couple of years after I 'hacked' into my then husband's email account, I was comfortable in my skin as a woman who had been informally separated for a two-year period. I was piecing my life back together, little by little. *One day at a time.* That was my mantra back then. *All I have to do is get through today,* I would say to myself. *That's all I have to do.* And get through the days, I did. It got better. As the months rolled by, I noticed that the dark cloud that seemed to be hovering over my head had lifted. The heaviness around my mouth (which made me feel as if I walked around with a perpetually downturned smile) began to disappear. I stepped out of my comfort zone – a job I had enjoyed and worked hard at for five years – and took on a new job with new challenges. I threw myself into proving myself on the job all over again. I was busier than ever, with family, with work, with church, with travel.

And then the FaceBook message came.

An old boyfriend of mine (whom I'll call 'Phillip') reached out to my sister via FB. They remained good friends even after we broke up, but had lost contact after some years and several relocations. All excited, my sister sent me an email with her full message in the subject heading: 'Phillip just contacted me on FB. Called and talked for two hours. Happily married with kids and doing really well. Asked about you. Still a REALLY nice guy!!'

I remember reading the subject line without surprise. I had known it would only be a matter of time.

I wasn't surprised, either, when an email from Phillip popped up in my inbox a couple of days later. I instantly reached for the phone and called my sister up.

"Did you give Phillip my email address?" I asked, like someone ready to pounce.

"No, absolutely not – and he never asked me for it, either."

"Oh … okay."

"He probably just Googled you. I don't understand what the big deal is, though. He's just an old friend and a really nice guy. Lighten up."

Famous last words.

I understood where she was coming from, though. I hadn't seen or heard from Phillip in almost two decades. We dated for two months or less when I was twenty years old. Our 'dating' consisted of his paying me intermittent visits at my sister's house for about two months, during which her entire household became enamored with him. He would follow me around patiently, as I cooked and did my chores, keeping up the conversation. She was right: he was a really nice guy – charming, polite, and amiable.

He was an unbeliever, too.

For that reason, I knew we could have no lasting relationship, but I was tempted to 'dabble.' The few believers I knew were so *booooring*, and I rationalized that at least he didn't seem turned off by spiritual things. The few Christian men I knew were young – meaning they were young in faith, too. They were still trying to figure out what Christianity meant for themselves, and this learning process often meant they were (or, at least seemed to me to be) hung up on the 'performance' of Christianity, for lack of a better term. As a result, few of them were well-rounded. My impression was that, for them, life wasn't necessarily God's Word as applied to living in the actual world – life *was* the Bible, and the Bible was life, period. There could be no other subject of conversation, and I found this stifling, unstimulating, and 'unreal.'

Conviction about my relationship with Phillip caught up with me about two months later, and I ended it, letting him know there couldn't be any future for us. We had actually talked about this repeatedly right from the beginning. We broke up and I didn't look back. I put myself back on the right path toward marrying someone that would share my faith.

I never heard from him again, until now. We had been two kids who knew nothing about life and only knew each other for a couple of months. How could communication between us, now that we were 'old folks' be anything but harmless?

In his email nearly twenty years later, he was very open about his curiosity about me. He wanted to know how I had been all this while. What my family was like. What my career was like. How life had treated me.

I replied his email carefully, trying to strike a balance between not sounding too excited, yet not sounding rude, either. *That should do it*, I said to myself. *Now, he knows about me and he can leave me alone. My sister can fill him in on the rest.*

But he replied.

And I was secretly glad.

'How are you?' he would ask. Innocent enough. But to a woman in as 'vulnerable' a position as I was at the time, this simple question was an absolute breath of fresh air – almost like life itself. *Someone actually wants to know how I am?* I would marvel. *How weird is that?*

'What did you have for lunch today? What time do you usually get to work? How did your meeting go? How are your children doing? What's your favorite thing to watch?'

I started looking forward to getting yet another email, with another set of seemingly innocent questions for me to respond to. *Whoa – steady, girl*, I would warn myself. *This is a happily married man, by his own admission. A married man, period.*

He apparently started going to church right after we broke up – ironically, he chose the same church I used to go to when visiting my sister back in those days. He considered himself a believer now – still trying to find his way, but a believer nonetheless. He was gainfully employed and the sole provider. He got married probably just a year before I did. I felt like gnashing my teeth, quite frankly.

Why am I telling this story?

I'm telling this story because I think it's important to openly share an important lesson I learned about just being human. Had it not nearly happened to me, I would never have realized that affairs (whether emotional or otherwise) can happen to anybody. Everybody is fair game. I'm the sort of person that, when emailing a man, would tend to carbon-copy his wife on the message, too, if I happened to know her. I was that careful about avoiding 'every appearance of evil' – and yet, provoked by a simple email message during a period of vulnerability, there I was, essentially becoming a 'strange woman' myself.

Although I never got answers from my former spouse, nor from any of 'the strange women,' through my own experience, I at least got some partial answers, a partial understanding of how easily all this can happen if one lets down one's guard for even a second.

Peggy Vaughan, who also experienced her spouse's infidelity (but whose marriage survived and actually became stronger), talks about this issue in her book, *The Monogamy Myth*:

> [T]here's a great deal of support in society for placing the entire blame on the person who succumbed to having an affair, regardless of the situation. Our tendency is to judge them quite harshly, seeing them as evil or 'sick' and in need of help to determine what caused them to do such a thing. We wonder why they bothered to get married if they didn't mean to be faithful, and we want to see them punished for what they did. We are self-righteous in our attitude because we're convinced they are deviant or immoral people. But in most instances, they are not bad people and don't deserve to be unilaterally blamed for what happened. While each of us is ultimately responsible for our behavior, the decision to have an affair doesn't take place in isolation; it is influenced by many other factors in society (pp. 19-20).

I finally understood just how easy it was to cross the line from reality to fantasy land.

How did I extricate myself from what very easily could have become one big mess?

The only way I knew how. By telling the truth. I told myself the truth and I told God the truth, which led me to tell my sisters the truth, and tell my friends the truth. "This is what's happening in my life," I would say, openly. "Pray for me because I don't want to do to anyone what others did to me. I know exactly how painful it is, and I can't believe I'm in this situation. But I am."

A few people brushed it off. "You're too uptight," they would say. "There's nothing wrong with just talking to an old friend."

"No," I would insist. "There is something wrong with it. I'm about to cross the line."

I told myself the truth.

"How can you cross the line with someone you haven't seen in two decades and probably never will see," some countered.

"It all starts in the heart," I would reply. "You may not be able to see my heart, but I can. And God can, too."

I knew that what a person like me needed to rise above this was a combination of practical and spiritual things. I had a couple of people standing with me in prayer. I read and meditated on Proverbs chapter 5 for many days, and took it seriously. Each time I read it, the dangerous path I was headed down became more and more vivid to me and stopped me in my tracks. I permanently deleted the emails.

And, I meditated on a movie. In the movie *A Beautiful Mind*, starring Russell Crowe and Jennifer Connelly and based on a true story, there's a scene that I will never forget, and that I continually apply to my life in many different areas. Russell Crowe plays a brilliant paranoid schizophrenic who's been convinced for years that his college roommate/best friend and the latter's niece are real. They follow him everywhere and he is absolutely unable to get rid of them, of this hallucination, even when he gets well enough to realize they're nothing but a figment of his imagination. When he does realize this, he makes the difficult decision to simply ignore them. The viewer watches these two characters, still following Russell Crowe's character around for his entire life, looking more and more wretched and despondent as he continues, by sheer determination, to *ignore* them over the years.

What I find so profound about this is that *they never left*. These two characters were like a *thorn* in the flesh, and there was no getting rid of them – not even when Russell Crowe's character finally won the Nobel Memorial Prize for Economics, in his old age.

The poignant lesson I derived from this movie is that, in life, there are some things you just have to learn to live with. In life, you can deal with your demons. In life, you can ignore things that aren't 'real', but that rear up their ugly heads once in a while, anyway. In life, you can ignore the potentially dangerous, enticing 'mirages' that come your way.

I have the mind of Christ, the Bible tells me, and by God, I'm going to act like it until I become it.

Yesterday, I marveled at the frailty of other human beings. Today, I am humbled by my own.

Do we dare judge?

When this book was still a blog, I received an interesting comment from an African, Christian reader who touched on the tension between 'not judging' a person's behavior and seeming permissive of unseemly behavior. As she pointed out, Christians are often admonished to refrain from judging others (Matthew 7:1) and to love their enemies (Matthew 5: 44). Some interpretations of these scriptures can promote abusive behavior in marriages, if we're not careful. Abusive spouses can capitalize on Bible verses such as these, and believe that they are never supposed to be called out on their behavior.

It's natural to want to judge the 'erring party' in a failed marriage. But I think that, for people who will one day judge angels (I Corinthians 6: 3), Christians need a lot more practice in carrying out judgments.

I don't think the term 'judge' always has to be seen as a dirty word. The Bible encourages us – *commands* us, really – to judge ourselves. To do continuous self-assessments so that others don't have to. It also encourages us to 'judge' (in my mind, meaning 'assess' or 'appraise') each other, when necessary, within the household of faith.

What business is it of mine to judge those outside the church?
Are you not to judge those inside? (I Corinthians 5: 12)

Those that profess Christianity are definitely held to a higher
standard.

But judgment has a unique and important purpose: to make the
one being assessed *better*. This should be the envisioned goal.
Not to make *ourselves* feel better, or to carry out a vendetta, or
to subconsciously protect some part of ourselves.

The problem with most judgments (when we pronounce them)
is that they tend to be more about *us* and the instant gratification
that can be derived from giving our opinion about the person
being judged.

Do we dare judge?

I think things have been set up so that we have no choice but
to judge sometimes, and these periodic judgments are essential.
When done properly, it is the responsible thing to do – to judge
ourselves with the goal of self-improvement, and to judge
others with the goal of their improvement in mind, too. To do
so properly, though, a full set of information is required – and
that's the tricky part.

I used to really hate appraisals at work. They come around every
year, the same time of the year. I hate appraising others and I
hate being appraised even more. I hate being 'judged.' But it's
so necessary. I have to admit that the knowledge that I will be
appraised helps me focus on what's important and makes me
work better. And the fact that the appraisal process is actually
pretty fair (and that all the information necessary to finalize the

appraisal is thoroughly utilized) always makes me determined to do better the next year. Rather than break my spirit, it makes me expect more of myself, want more for myself.

I think that's what 'judgment' should look like.

In a court of law

I'm not sure what I expected.

Maybe something akin to *Kramer vs. Kramer*. Except I wasn't Meryl Streep and this was no movie.

I had never been in a Nigerian court before. I really didn't know what to expect.

I'm a *Law and Order* kind of girl. I watched all three versions when I had access to all three versions. I got a kick out of watching *The Practice* and almost any other kind of show that had anything to do with a courtroom. Given my fascination with the way the law works, it's a wonder that it never occurred to me to become a lawyer. (The thought never even crossed my mind.)

I had just met my lawyer in person for the first time a couple of days earlier. Prior to this, we had only communicated on the phone and via email. I imagined him as a tall, skinny, light-skinned man with glasses. He turned out to be a tall, heavyset, dark-skinned man with glasses.

On the D-day, he drove to the courthouse with his associate seated next to him and me in the back. His radio blared out loud, vernacular Christian music. He sang along and intermittently took his hands off the steering wheel to clap loudly. I got the sense that he was psyching himself up for his appearance in court.

I sat in a spot a couple of rows from the very back of the courtroom. We had arrived early and there were a number of cases that needed to be heard before mine.

The first involved a nun. I couldn't quite tease out what her offence was. All I know is that she wasn't there, and so I watched the lawyers (in their white wigs and black cloaks) go at it in her absence. The judge demanded an explanation for the nun's tardiness.

"My Lord," her lawyer explained, "She lives very far away and must be caught in traffic."

With that, he made a quick, comical, jeering face at the opposing counsel.

"My Lord," the opposing counsel countered, "In that case, he should have mentioned this to me. I live on that side of town and would have gladly given his client a ride."

He stuck out his tongue at the nun's lawyer and they both stifled their chuckles.

The judge sat up on the dais with his head bowed throughout this exchange as he calmly wrote out his notes in long hand. He seemed totally oblivious to the lawyers' antics.

Sitting behind the lawyers, I had a good vantage point and I watched the scene before me in absolute amazement. The next case came up and the lawyers poked even more fun at each other, while the judge remained oblivious, fixated as he was on taking down copious notes. Despite my shock, I watched the lawyers with a bit of admiration. They were clearly so comfortable and confident handling these legal issues, that this was almost like fun to them. At the same time, I really hoped they knew what they were doing.

There was a young man sitting in what would be the stenographer's seat (if this were *Law and Order*). He slept soundly almost from the time I entered the courtroom to the time I left. I wondered what his role was supposed to be, since there was no stenograph machine in sight, and the judge was patiently writing everything out himself with a pen and paper.

Somewhere along the line, my husband entered the courtroom and sat on the opposite side of the room. Maybe this was *Kramer vs. Kramer* after all.

As a new hearing began with different lawyers, my lawyer ushered us all out for a brief meeting. I exchanged greetings with my husband and his lawyer. "Look," my lawyer stressed, "This case is about desertion. The divorce was filed on those grounds and I want you both to remember that when you're called up to the witness stand."

"The real reason why she filed for divorce is because she believes I was involved with a friend of hers. That's the real reason why we're here today," my soon-to-be-ex-husband asserted.

"Well, I don't know anything about that, so I don't know what you're talking about. All I know is what my client has told me and we all know the grounds upon which this case was filed.

147

Let's not complicate this case by bringing in last-minute stories," my lawyer replied with a tinge of irritation in his voice.

My husband had his response ready: "Well, let's just pray that the judge doesn't ask me what *I* want, because if he does, I'll tell him. I didn't marry her to divorce her."

As my lawyer advised the opposing counsel to try and reign in his client, I pulled my husband aside and said, "Look. I've spent a lot of money on this whole process. This is money I should have reserved for the children's needs. Do *not* mess things up for me after I've come all this way."

He laughed.

Was he mocking me?

I decided to walk away and hope for the best. We had discussed the divorce a long time ago and had come to an agreement that we would move forward with it. We had sat together for two hours, pouring over and filling out the paper work when we thought we were going to file in a different country. Then, I realized how tricky that would be and we changed the location of the court proceedings. We had talked about this and ironed everything out. I wasn't prepared to stomach any surprises.

It was our turn now – the last hearing for the day. I noticed that a couple of lawyers who had been glancing back at me curiously decided to wait behind to learn more about my case.

I took the stand and my lawyer asked a series of strategic questions to which I responded. How long had we been separated? When was the last time he paid a bill for me or the children? How much had he spent on us in the last decade? Who took care of all the children's needs? What was my understanding of why his financial support ceased? Before the separation, how many times in a year did the children and I see him? What was the reason for his limited presence? Etc., etc., etc.

The judge was from northern Nigeria. He came across as compassionate, wise, and a good listener, while still maintaining professional distance. I silently thanked God. He had to keep telling me, though, to slow down and repeat myself. I kept forgetting that he was actually writing down everything I had to say.

My lawyer was done and the opposing counsel took over with another battery of questions: When was the last time your husband came to visit again? During his last few visits, where did he lodge? Since he stayed in your home, where did he sleep? Are you trying to say that all these years, you've not had sexual relations with him even though he stays in your home when he visits? Where does he eat when he visits? Since he eats in your home when he visits, who prepares the food? So you mean you still prepare food for your husband and you want to divorce him?

My lawyer objected. "My Lord, my client has said she prepares food for the whole household and everyone is free to eat what is prepared, including the father of her children. Does he expect my client to starve him?"

This was simply hilarious. I held onto my poker face, though, and ignored the giggles welling up inside me. This was a serious matter. I could laugh about the comical parts later.

My former husband's lawyer calmed down and asked gently: "Are you saying that my client has contributed nothing to your life? Are you saying that you've never annoyed my client?"

What's that got to do with anything? I gave some polite answer and was finally allowed to take my seat.

It was his turn to take the stand. The exact questions he was asked are all a blur now. All I recall are some of his responses – or, rather, some of his statements which were tangential to the questions being posed.

I didn't marry her to get divorced ...

The real reason why she's divorcing me is because some people made up some lies about me and her friend ...

I cringed and so did my lawyer and his associate. Their faces fell and they began pinching each other in consternation. My lawyer tried to object, but the judge waved him away. He wanted to hear what the man had to say. He listened patiently and took down his notes.

I squirmed in my seat, restraining myself from standing up. I wanted to find out from my lawyer if I could get back on the witness stand. I wanted to correct some of the half-truths that were being told about various issues. I knew my lawyer wouldn't welcome my moving around in the courtroom, though, so I made myself sit down and shut up.

In the end, the judge put down his pen and looked at my husband.

"What do *you* want?'"

I was stunned. This was the very question he had said we'd better pray no one asked him.

We all held our breath during the pregnant pause that followed. You could hear a pin drop in the courtroom.

He finally gave a long, convoluted answer.

"I'm going to give you another chance," the judge said. "In simple terms, what do *you* want out of all this?"

My soon-to-be-ex-husband paused again, this time for a longer period.

Finally, he said, "This is not necessarily what I would have wanted, but I want to give her what she wants. I want whatever she wants."

My lawyers and I heaved a collective sigh of relief. I really hoped that the judge was satisfied.

Both lawyers conferred with the judge to set another date to appear in court a couple of months later.

As we walked out of the courtroom, my lawyer said, "We're done. You won't have to make another trip down here for this again."

"What? You mean, it's all over?"

"Yes."

"Seriously?" I couldn't believe it.

"Yes. You don't have to be here for the final decree. I'll send you the papers when they're ready."

"Wow .... Thank you ..."

I turned to my children's father and we stood together for a few seconds outside the courthouse. "Thank you for not making this more difficult for me than it could have been."

He shook his head. "I didn't marry you to make things difficult for you."

Could've fooled me!

I'm such a meanie sometimes. But that's how I felt.

As I walked back to my lawyer's car, the other lawyers that had waited behind out of curiosity walked by me.

"Best of luck, Madam," they said warmly.

"Thank you so much," I replied, touched.

From here on out, I was going to need all the luck I could get.

Intolerable behavior

I didn't take the time to read through my divorce decree until over a year after the divorce was final. When I first received it, all I did was skim through it. Prior to receiving it, I wondered what it would look like. I had asked my lawyer several times when I was going to get my 'divorce certificate' and he kept assuring me it was coming. And so, I guess I expected to receive an actual 'certificate' much like my marriage certificate. My divorce decree turned out to be a twelve-page document that I decided to read later. I was just so relieved at the time to have put the legal part of the divorce behind me that I couldn't be bothered with other details. *I was there in the courtroom, after all*, I told myself. *I know exactly what happened.*

When I finally read the document carefully for the first time, I was surprised by some of the things I found. I read the divorce decree word for word, and then re-read it. It's not that anything was misrepresented, or anything like that. It's just that reading the document brought home the politics of divorce – of the legal process surrounding the dissolution of a marriage, that is.

I filed for divorce on grounds of desertion. From the internet research I carried out before getting a lawyer, there are apparently several grounds for divorce in Nigeria, and I wasn't terribly comfortable with any of them. After giving it a lot of thought, though, 'desertion' seemed to be something I could work with. I recall that my lawyer made an effort to carefully steer me away from the grounds of 'adultery,' explaining that it would be too complicated to pursue a case on those grounds. I was actually relieved and assured him that I didn't want to get into that, anyway. It felt really weird, though, to have to try and 'squeeze' myself, my situation, into one little box in order to be able to get a divorce. The issues leading up to a divorce are usually so much more complex than that, and so having to choose a few boxes out of an already limited set of options leaves one with a feeling that the process is 'incomplete.'

I went along with it, nonetheless, with the ultimate goal in mind. I reasoned that 'desertion' didn't sound as bad as some of the other grounds. I rationalized that there was indeed a subtle form of desertion involved, as I was on my own practically all the time, solely supporting myself and the children. I gave up more and more parts of my spouse because it really seemed like he felt stifled by marriage. He would repeatedly make comments about the things he wouldn't hold back from, the risks he would take (professionally) 'if I were not married.' So I released more and more of him in order for him not to feel caged in. These and other things amounted to what I could feel comfortable calling a subtle form of 'desertion.'

As I write this, I remember that an in-law of mine asked a couple of times (in the early years of the marriage) why I didn't just pack up and move – move over to the country to which my husband had relocated. I explained that I wasn't opposed to it, but that I didn't get any invitations from him to prompt such a decision. My residing where I did was a joint decision made for pragmatic reasons, so I couldn't just up and move with kids. It's not like my partner was begging (or even asking) me to join him. He was as 'pragmatic' as I was: Where would we live? *How* would we live? We had a good, predictable life where we were; why exchange that for the unknown?

Maybe my in-law was onto something, though. Maybe where and how we would live should not have been a concern of mine. There is a chance that if I had relocated without a plan, he would have been forced to make one. Then again, there is also a chance that I would have regretted not having a plan very deeply in the end, given my personality. I honestly didn't have the liver to leave a stable job and move to another country, not knowing what our source of income would be.

And so, 'desertion' it was. Plus, my lawyer threw in the fact that we'd been separated for well over three years (which apparently is a big deal in Nigerian law), along with 'intolerable behavior,' for good measure.

What I didn't realize (until I read the divorce decree) was that my former husband cross-petitioned for the dissolution of the marriage on the grounds of the over-three-year separation, plus on the grounds of 'intolerable conduct.' In other words, we were each claiming the other had behaved in such a manner that we could not reasonably be expected to live with each other.

Except that's not what we were really saying.

We were obligated to say 'something' and we relied on our lawyers to say it for us. Our lawyers spoke the language that the law understands, even if it may not have been a completely accurate reflection of what we wanted to say. I suppose each of us could sincerely accuse the other of 'intolerable behavior,' but, in my mind, the legal dissolution of the marriage really wasn't about pegging the end of a fifteen-year marriage down to one thing. It was about knowing the marriage was no more, but needing to bring it to an end in the eyes of others, too. Much as I would have liked to be able to choose exactly how to end it legally, this was not an available option. And so, whatever needed to be done in the eyes of the law, needed to be done.

Although my husband had resolved within himself to grant me the divorce, apparently, the law wouldn't let him do that. He had to put up at least some show of resistance.

In the end, the judge remained unconvinced.

From carefully reading the divorce decree, I learned that the judge considered both of our claims (or, rather, our lawyers' claims) of intolerable behavior to be hogwash. Ironically, despite the concerted efforts on both of our parts (or, rather, on our lawyers' parts) to cram ourselves into the boxes available to us by law, the divorce was granted for one, refreshingly simple reason: We had been separated for at least two years, and neither of us had disagreed on this fact.

The judge decided none of us had evidence to prove any of our other claims. I couldn't prove 'desertion' any more than he could prove 'intolerable behavior.' In his exact, eloquent words:

'Since in the instant case the Petitioner had led no evidence in respect of those averments, I must deem them as abandoned. For this reason the Petitioner's allegation of intolerable behavior against the Respondent has failed.'

As I blinked and re-read this portion of the document, my initial impression of this judge as a good one who knew his stuff was reaffirmed.

I thought about this for a couple of minutes – the fact that the judge didn't even buy the 'desertion' argument. I searched myself to gauge the extent to which this mattered to me.

I decided that it didn't matter.

When I made up my mind to file for divorce, I didn't want a 'blame game' (we had had almost four years of separation to do that, after all, if that were a priority). I just wanted a divorce. But in contexts where no such thing as a 'no-contest' divorce exists, you are obligated to play the blame game, whether you want to or not.

In the end, I was just glad that I didn't go through all the red tape in vain. The process may not have been what I really wanted (nor what I fully understood – I mean, I still don't understand why, when I was filing, being separated for over three years wasn't enough grounds, but in the end, it turned out to be exactly enough!), but the outcome was satisfactory.

In the grand scheme of things, that's all that really counts.

Where is my anger?

In her book *Falling Apart in One Piece: One Optimist's Journey Through the Hell of Divorce*, Stacy Morrison tells the story of how, in frustration one day, her sister-in-law asked her where her anger was. How come she was anything but totally outraged by the fact that her husband woke up one day, and, for no clear reason under the sun, decided he was 'done.' I have essentially been asked the same question by a number of people who have wondered if I was 'for real.'

Among the gamut of emotions I have gone through over the last few years, anger has rarely ever made it to the top five. I don't have a complete sense of why, but I can see how its lack of prominence can be puzzling for some.

In sifting through my memories, I do remember one scene in which I starred as the angry lead.

I hadn't had much to say in months. And then, I had to go home for a memorial event in honor of my father. After that, I spent the next few days travelling by road from city to city at a frenetic pace, trying to ensure I saw my mother-in-law and other in-laws before I left the country again. We were still legally married at this time, although it didn't feel like it. He and his brothers made sure they personally chauffeured me around from state to state (bless their hearts).

Maybe it was the combination of being on the road and in a different city every day, and the emotional stress of attending this memorial event; on my last day in town, I just flipped. I felt seriously provoked by his attempt to cover up his real feelings with what I saw as deceit and a show of cockiness.

"Do you think this is a joke?" I yelled, not caring who heard. "You'd better go get yourself tested for HIV and put this charade aside!"

He and his brother stared back at me – his brother, in utter shock, and him … well, I couldn't read his expression clearly.

"You know what?" I continued, wanting badly to hit below the belt. "My father wasn't a perfect man. So why d'you think everybody is so torn up by his death? Why do you think people travelled from far and near after all this time to honor him? I'll tell you why: he wasn't a perfect man, but he was a principled man. He was an honest man," I spat out at him while he walked out in annoyance for a few seconds. As he walked back in, I turned to his brother and said pointedly in a dangerously quiet tone: "The last time I slept with your brother was in February 2008. I will NEVER sleep with your brother again."

My poor brother-in-law stood in the middle of the room staring helplessly at me, not sure whether to be embarrassed, sympathetic, or upset. None of my in-laws had ever heard so much as a peep out of me before, and they didn't know what to make of this ugly, livid creature. Most of them were used to a woman that smiled and laughed and joked all the time. I don't think I've ever talked as much in my life as I talked that day. I needed to get it all out and I did just that.

Long story short: have I had an angry moment or two? Absolutely. Could I be more outraged over the turn of events? Absolutely.

And if I'm not, then there are several good reasons why.

First, I was in a weak, sick, dysfunctional marriage, and so I was more inclined to embrace the chance to live healthier – even if it meant I would no longer be married. Why be perpetually angry over what could very well turn out to be a new lease on life?

Second, I honestly feel I have so much to be grateful for that living in anger really seems pointless. I'm writing this on an airplane and, as I usually do on long-haul flights, I've spent some time watching a movie – *Kramer vs. Kramer*. The first time I ever watched it, I was seven years old and I watched it with my father. All these years later, it remains a timeless classic – as poignant now as it was then. It reminded me of the fact that I got a divorce with absolutely no custody battle. Now, if that's not something to rejoice over, then I don't know what is. I walked away with my everyday life intact and with my children to share it with me.

I don't receive spousal support, but I don't have to pay any, either. Not every person in my position is this fortunate. I don't get child support, either, and I did not ask for any. I didn't want a big fight; I just wanted to be able to move on peacefully. I'm also convinced that no matter what is or isn't written down on paper, a real father will be concerned about and want to contribute toward his children's upkeep. And at some point, I had to accept reality: my children's father was either 'real' or not, and whichever he was, my children would not suffer. Although it would be nice to have this sort of support for my children, thankfully, I do not need it. My life and the children's lives have not changed without it, and that is a super-duper blessing, if you ask me.

I don't have to rearrange my children's lives, or mine, in any significant way because their father lives in a different country. We are all spared the agony of having to shuttle the children back and forth between two homes. Another reason not to be angry.

I would definitely have been devastated had I been a stay-at-home mom (which I was once) when all of this happened. I'm thankful that it happened at a point in my life when I could make a particular decision because I *wanted* to, rather than being compelled to make a different decision for financial reasons. Few women are that fortunate. I could go on and on and on ... but you get my drift.

Third: because this book focuses on divorce (a 'negative' event), it is hard for an outsider looking in to have a sense of my former spouse's 'good' side. As an insider, I'm privy to the 'bad' and the 'ugly' aspects of this failed union, but also to the 'good.' In earlier years, the positive aspects of my ex-husband's character actually convinced me that I was 'marrying up.' It's unfortunate that the 'good' wasn't enough to overwhelm the other aspects. The stark contrast between what was then, and what is now, persuades me that something is not quite 'right.' But whatever that 'something' is, I finally had to accept that as much as I once wanted to and tried to, it was not my job to remedy it. It was his.

Fourth and finally: If I'm going to spend my life angry at him, then I necessarily have to spend my life angry at myself, too.

Did he do a lot of things that I'd like to strangle him for? Sure. But out of all the people in the world, out of all of my suitors, I chose him. To be fair, I should also be angry at myself for not making a different choice, for not being wise enough, for not putting myself in a position to be wiser, etc., etc., etc.

The problem is that I don't have the wherewithal to beat myself up forever, and I'm certainly not going to spend all that energy doing this to someone else.

The last time I said 'I love you'

I meant it when I said it.

It was February 29th, four years before my divorce. The date is important.

I found out about the affair with my friend in January that year. The period between that time and the end of February seemed like a lifetime. Not only because the days were slow and painful, but also because a myriad of events occurred during that period that made it increasingly clear to me that the relationship would not, *could* not survive.

The metaphor of a burning house comes to mind again when I think about this.

To be fair, I suppose there are at least a couple of ways to react to your house bursting into flames. Some might instinctively run in, despite the obvious danger, and at least save *something* – helpless children, family albums, important documents, a stash of cash. ... Others might simply (and understandably) be completely paralyzed by fear. The fear, understandably, can lead to the cover-up – and without care, the cover-up becomes such an important mission that it outweighs the fear and eventually metamorphosizes into something entirely different in character. The fear with which one started out is then completely forgotten.

The date is important because it represents the time soon after I burst into tears in front of one of the other women with my husband present. It represents countless other times when he had a chance ('big' chances and 'little' chances) to make things right – or even to just feebly attempt to make things right ... and didn't ... and somehow expected that normal married life would miraculously go on as usual. It represents the multiple times that he didn't fight for me, for *us*, when he could have.

February 29th was a Friday. It was the last Friday of the month, meaning there was a night vigil service at church. He attended the night vigil service while I stayed home. He left the service early, though, and came back home. I was awakened by his movement as he entered the room, and I watched his silhouette in the darkness for a few minutes. Without a word, he confidently drew me close, ready to share intimacy.

I wasn't sure what I wanted. I had spent the last couple of months disgusted with him, shunning him, and cringing at the very thought of any physical contact. He finally came to accept that I would not let him touch me. This night, however, he was suddenly filled with an unusual measure of boldness – perhaps inspired by the couple of hours he had spent in prayer.

This night, I hated him and I didn't hate him. I was hurt and I almost understood. I wanted to hurt him back and I wanted to take all our unnecessary pain and turmoil away. I wanted to be rid of him and I wanted my husband back.

The intimacy over and his arm around me, he murmured to himself as much as to the invisible interlocutor: "Devil, I deserve her ..."

I wished I was privy to the rest of that conversation. Years of experience had taught me that I would not be allowed in on it, though. And so I lay there, guessing at what he meant; wondering what kind of torment he was experiencing, if any; wondering if this conversation with the devil gave him any sort of real assurance.

"I love you," he said – this time, to me.

I paused for a few seconds, searching myself and trying to ascertain how I really felt. It took several seconds for me to wade through the confusion, the grief, the disbelief, the ruins.

Finally certain, I replied: "I love you, too."

In that moment, I meant it. I did love the person I thought I had originally married. But I meant something else, too.

There was a satisfied silence from his end and he fell asleep. I remained awake, with my last words to him hanging in the air.

That was the last time I said it and the last time we touched.

I really do believe I meant it in that moment. When I uttered the word 'love,' I meant it in the true sense of the word. In that moment, it wasn't about what he had or hadn't done. It was no longer about his 'record of wrongs.' As the Bible says, 'Love is patient, love is kind. It does not envy, it does not boast, it is not self-seeking, it is not easily angered, it keeps not record of wrongs. Love does not delight in evil but rejoices with the truth. It always protects, always trusts, always hopes, always perseveres' (I Corinthians 13: 1-7).

When I said, 'I love you,' I meant (as I'm sure God means, too): I *see* you. And what I see does not change how I feel about you. I forgive you. You hurt me, but I do not hate you. I release you. I almost understand you – and even if I never end up fully doing so, that's okay. You are still worthy as a child of God saved by grace. In God's eyes, and in mine.

I had a taste, in that brief moment, of what God's love for us all must be like. And yet, as unfathomable as God's love is (Ephesians 3: 17-19), it is not cheap. Being allowed into God's circle of love, and being allowed to remain there, comes with certain conditions.

The man that I married would wake up the following morning, puzzled by my aloofness given what had transpired the night before. I did not explain. So much had gone unexplained between us for so long. This was just one more thing that wouldn't make a difference.

Although I didn't realize it until after the fact, the last time I said 'I love you' … I was saying good-bye.

Just because

I'm not sure if it's traveling that I don't like, or if it's just that I don't like being away from my kids – which usually happens when I travel since most of my trips are work-related. I suspect I just don't like traveling, though.

Nonetheless, I've noticed that there's something about traveling and being in another country for a short while that has an almost spiritual effect on me sometimes. Once in a while, it happens while the plane is landing and I'm in my seat, looking out the window. As I land in countries I've only read about, I sometimes have an overwhelming feeling of awe at God's greatness, and at the fact that He's made it possible for me to visit a number of these places.

And then, there's the *quietness* of the hotel rooms. I'm so used to being surrounded by commotion and demands, that being in a hotel room in the middle of nowhere, all by myself, draws me closer to God sometimes. To combat the feelings of guilt about leaving my children behind, and the loneliness of hotel rooms (as opposed to my own home), I turn to God and feel a special kind of intimacy.

On one particular trip last year, I was moved by three things: the thick, heavy quietness of my hotel room, a movie, and a news clip.

The movie was a true story (which are my favorite kind) – the simple but touching story of an unemployed, African-American woman. A single parent in a low-income neighborhood, she courageously stood up against the entire police force, with all the odds against her, and successfully drew national attention to the discrimination often faced by the urban poor.

I was profoundly touched by this simple movie. To crown it all, I switched to CNN and discovered it was Archbishop Desmond Tutu's 80th birthday. He was being interviewed, along with his family members and others, and his contributions to the fight against apartheid were expertly chronicled. I was in complete awe of what God can do with our lives if we just let Him. The thought of these two people, coupled with the quietness of my room, led me to tears. I had a strong urge to just worship the Lord in the quietness of my room, marveling at all He is able to do. I decided to just worship Him for a few minutes, just because. I don't do this nearly enough.

I was relieved to be heading home the following evening, and this, too, probably played a part in making me so emotional.

The following day, my flight had some ridiculous delays. As we learned that the flight had been delayed yet again, after having waited a couple of hours already, I exchanged exasperated glances with the lady sitting next to me. We struck up a conversation and eventually began to converse like old friends. She was a young American lady doing some de-mining work in an insecure African location. I stared at her admiringly while she talked about her work, nodded understandingly, as she talked about her family challenges. We made our way to a café and had some pizza together, continuing our conversation for another couple of hours.

"Are you signed up with this whole frequent flyer mile thing?" she asked.

"Yes, I am – are you?"

"No," she said.

"Oh, you should definitely sign up, especially given how much you travel. There are quite a number of benefits." I described the application process as we finally stood in line, waiting to board.

It was my turn now, so I handed the flight attendant my boarding pass.

"Have you ever traveled business class?" she asked, standing behind me.

"Very rarely," I replied, turning around to look at her. "And the very few times it's happened, I was upgraded because my boss went up to the counter and sweet-talked the flight attendants."

Just then, there was a resounding beep as my boarding pass went through the machine. I quickly turned back to the flight attendant, slightly panicked. I couldn't bear to have anything else happen tonight. I just wanted to get home.

"Is there something wrong?" I asked apprehensively.

"Oh, no," he said, casually. "We're just upgrading you to business class. Enjoy your flight."

I turned back and stared at my airport friend, eyes wide and mouth open. She stared back with surprise and a touch of envy. I said my goodbyes hurriedly, apologetically, and left her behind.

Oh my God, I thought as I settled in my large, comfortable seat. *Poverty is terrible. You mean some people actually get to travel this way all the time?? Thank you Lord, for this privilege. I'm just so shocked. This has never happened to me without any 'manipulation.'*

I had some juice and then began to doze off, lulled into a light sleep by the buzz of the air conditioning. I was awakened from this sweet sleep by someone standing beside me in the aisle, obviously trying to get into the seat next to mine.

"Excuse me, Mum," the voice said, gently. I looked up and stared. Then I wiped my eyes to be sure I wasn't dreaming. His sharp, alert, kind eyes stared patiently back at me. I nearly fell out of my seat.

Guess who it was?

ARCHBISHOP DESMOND TUTU!

My shock and hesitancy didn't go unnoticed by those around me. They were equally awe-struck, but a bit amused by what I would call my '*bushmalism.*' I finally gathered myself together and stood out in the aisle while he moved past me and took his seat. As he did so, I wasn't sure what to say. I couldn't just not say anything, like a bush girl. And so, I said the first thing that came to mind:

"Happy 80th Birthday, Bishop …"

"Oh, *thank you*, my dear. Thank you so much," he said graciously, humbly.

Thank *God* I'd watched CNN the previous night. *Okay, so what should I say next?* I wondered. *Should I strike up a conversation? About what, though?* I kept trying to catch a better glimpse of him out of the corner of my left eye. I noticed he was trying to get the attention of the flight attendant to hang up his coat.

"Let me take that for you," I offered.

"Oh, no, no – don't worry. He'll come get it eventually" – which he did.

I sat uncomfortably in my ultra-comfortable seat, wishing for a few minutes that I had my sister's personality. She would definitely know what to say (probably even exchange business cards) and have a great story to tell later. I said nothing further.

A few minutes later, I was glad I didn't strike up a conversation. Archbishop Desmond Tutu had fallen into a deep sleep right beside me, totally ignoring his dinner.

The plane landed in the morning. "You have to say *something* before you get off," I told myself. 'These things don't happen every day.'

And so as I grabbed my laptop, I said, "I'm really honored to have sat next to you on this flight. I hope you enjoy your stay."

"Thank you. Thank you, my dear," he replied graciously, clearly used to the effect he has on people.

He was ushered off the flight and met by a group of protocol people at the end of the hall.

It's interesting to me to see how I had this wonderful, memorable experience that I will always treasure, just because I was in the presence of this remarkable man. Some would say that this is what a marriage is supposed to be like, and perhaps that was even one of the intentions: that women and men would be enthralled by the very presence of their spouses. I suppose a major challenge here is having women and men do what it takes to keep their spouses enthralled – to care enough to do so – and for their efforts to matter to the one on the receiving end.

When I got home and switched on the TV, Archbishop Desmond Tutu was on, officiating over a ceremony. I was doubly glad I hadn't disturbed his sleep. The poor man had walked off the plane and right into a high-profile event.

I knelt down by my bedside. *Thank you, Lord*, I said.

I was convinced that God deliberately did me a special favor. Deliberately wanted to show me His greatness and His ability. He just wanted to 'rub it in' a bit and remind me of His incomparably great power. Just to make me feel special, just to let me know He's there. I can't explain how I'm sure, but I just *know* God was letting me know He's with me, He's watching, He's caring.

He did it just because.

Guess who's coming to dinner?

My sister thinks I need to see a psychologist.

Maybe she's right. The Nigerian in me silently scoffs at the idea, though.

I can read about co-dependency, etc., on my own (thank God for Google!), my internal Naija voice says.

My Nigerian voice aside, though, and despite my real respect for the psychology profession, I remain unconvinced.

"You need a psychologist to help you figure out why you have this need to be so 'nice' to your ex-husband," she insists. Perhaps she has a point.

My former husband came over about a week ago for a ten-day visit. He hadn't seen the children in almost two years. I'm guessing that there are two reasons for this: one is financial, as his business endeavors don't seem to have turned out too well over the years. The other, I think, probably has to do with the fact that it's hard to come back to a place that used to be home when you know it's not quite 'home' anymore. It's hard to move from being a king in your castle to an 'ordinary' visitor in someone else's. The combination of these two things plausibly makes it almost easier to just stay away.

"I don't think I'm being 'nice,' though, necessarily," I say to my sister. "I'm just being 'me.' This divorce thing is new for me and new for him. If there's a manual on how to do it 'right,' I haven't read it yet. I'm just taking things one day at a time and doing what feels right to me at any given time."

When the marriage was in the throes of death, taking its last breaths (we were informally separated at the time), things got to a point where it became critical for me to have him find his own accommodation when he visited the children. I achieved this only once (if only for a couple of days), and this was the last time the children saw him until now. Back then, I really didn't like the sort of person I had become as a result of the downward spiral of the marriage. I had become a master sleuth. I became a pro at hurriedly going through his cell phones (which he – an ordinarily not-too-careful individual – had begun to guard like a hawk all of the sudden) to see which calls and text messages had come in and gone out. It was hard to get a hold of his cell phones as he had also become a pro at not letting them out of his sight. I have a vivid memory, though (seems a bit comical now), of walking into the bathroom of the master bedroom and finding, to my great surprise, that he had actually forgotten them in there.

I methodically locked myself in the bathroom, sat down on the commode, and took my sweet time going through his phones. I heard him rush back to the bedroom in a panic, trying to figure out where he had left them. Not finding them, he rushed out to another room. When I was done, I casually told him that he'd left them in the bathroom, ensuring my voice and eyes didn't give away the fact that I'd just 'invaded' his privacy. I was rarely 'disappointed' with my findings on the rare occasions when I did get a hold of his phones, and trying to reconcile the text messages and phone logs with the person I thought I had married was the most confusing thing in the world.

I wasn't proud of my newly-acquired 'private investigator' skills, though. I loathed the fact that I was no longer myself – the fact that *I*, an ultra-busy individual who could barely keep up with her own email, and who would never have even thought of checking *his* email (not even in those days when I had his password), would now actually take the time to sift through his messages, trying to figure out what on *earth* was going on. *Me*, a professional at minding my own business and giving people space – I suddenly found the time and energy to care about who was calling and texting who?

I couldn't *stand* the new me. And because all this went totally against my nature, his one-week visits would totally exhaust me. Upon his departure, I would invariably fall ill – totally spent – and it would take me about another week to recover.

During one of these visits, I fell asleep around 8 p.m. with a blinding headache. It was the end of the one-week visit and he was leaving early the next morning. I fell asleep thinking drowsily about how familiar this had all become – the sudden, terrible headache and my falling ill just as he was getting ready to depart. The headache was a sign that the visit was over and that it was time for my body to rebel again and go out of whack for another week or so while it fought to rid itself of my pent-up emotions.

I woke up from sleep with a start a few hours later, awakened by my son, who had ran into the bathroom of the master bedroom with his Daddy's phone ringing loudly. My son noisily announced to his Dad who the caller was.

It was one of the 'strange women' – a cherished friend.

The bedroom light was off, and the bright light from the bathroom worsened my headache. My son's father took the phone without a word and let it ring and ring until the caller gave up. *Why doesn't he pick it up?* I wondered. *Does he realize I'm awake?* My hand felt around in the darkness for my phone and I looked at the time. It was a few minutes to 11 p.m.

At 10:58 p.m. that night, I decided that I would not let this happen to me again. I would not allow this to continue to be my life.

I later told him to kindly make his own accommodation arrangements when next he was visiting. "The way you decide to live your life is really your own business," I said. "But when it begins to affect my health, then it becomes my business. Do whatever you want, but please do it within your own space."

With his recent visit last week – his first visit since the divorce – these memories came back to me.

I compare how I felt back then to how I feel now. I find that everything has totally changed. I've totally 'moved on.' I no longer feel the urge to know what's going on in his life, to dig into his business. We're not married anymore, and so that feeling has completely dissipated. I'm back to being me again – the ultra-busy person who doesn't have time to sweat the 'small' stuff. In fact, I had actually forgotten all about my accommodation 'rule' until he (and then my sister!) reminded me. The rule came about as a result of a specific set of circumstances, which no longer exist. He was now here for the sole reason of spending time with his children, who hadn't seen him in forever, and – call me crazy – but I saw no reason why I shouldn't do whatever I could to facilitate this.

I think I'm just doing what feels most comfortable to me in any given moment. If I'm being 'nice' here, then I guess I'm being nice to our children, who deserve the best that I can possibly give them. Why do I 'allow' all this? Why would I agree to let him reside with us for ten days in a year; grant him the luxury of feeling free to eat whatever he wants; the comfort of a clean, safe place to stay, even though I know he hasn't planned to leave a penny behind for the upkeep of the children?

Because, for now, it works for me this way. It works for me and for the children.

He gave me a day's notice when he was coming, or else I would've tried to fix up the visitor's room for him. We moved recently and now have a vacant visitor's bedroom that I've done nothing with yet. So he slept in our son's room the whole time. There's a bunk bed in our son's room. Our daughter slept with her Daddy almost every night on the bottom bunk, while our son slept on the top. I gladly gave the 'three musketeers' their space and spent my nights in my own room across the hall, contentedly thinking of my two children getting their fill of their father.

"How does it all work out?" my pastor asked in fascination. "What's the atmosphere in the house like now that the marriage is over and he's back for a visit? What's it like for the children to see their parents sleep in two separate rooms?" He had a whole battery of interesting questions for me on Sunday, concerned about how we were all doing.

Actually, my daughter has never known anything else. The separation began when she was one, so she has no recollection of us ever sharing a room, and four years later, she's never asked why we don't. I guess he's just never here often enough for this to be a big issue for her. My son is old enough to understand the concept of divorce, and has gotten used to his father sharing a room with him during his rare visits, rather than with me, over the last four years. I tell my pastor that the atmosphere in the house is just fine. We're not enemies. We're quite civil to each other, actually.

With the ten-day visit now over and his father now gone, our son said to me tonight: "I'm glad that even though you're both divorced now, you're still respectful toward each other. You guys are just like acquaintances or something, and I'm glad you never fight or yell at each other, or anything like that."

The profound observation of this thirteen-year old moved me.

"Your dad and I don't hate each other," I reminded him gently. "The fact that we got divorced doesn't mean we're enemies. I may not fully understand him, but I don't hate him, and he's not a bad person. Even though I don't love him as a husband anymore, I still care about your dad. Things just didn't work out."

"Yeah, I know," he replied.

I suppose it's precious moments like this that make me want to be 'nice' – that is, to resist the occasional temptation to shut my former husband completely out of my life, and to instead do whatever I can to ensure my children have access to their father, and vice-versa. If my children can come out of this situation whole, knowing that their imperfect parents love them to death, and still knowing that God is good, then I've fulfilled my purpose and fulfilled it well, despite the circumstances.

The complications remain, though. My former spouse was in church with us last Sunday and the Sunday before that. I couldn't exactly tell him to find himself another church (although the thought did cross my mind, and he actually alluded to this possibility himself. I may take him up on this offer the next time – but I suppose that would be unfair). When a relatively new member of the church mentioned that he had met 'my spouse' at last, I had to correct him and point out that we were no longer married.

"Oh, that explains it," he said. "I was wondering why Pastor introduced him as your children's father, rather than simply as your husband."

I laughed.

"Pastor was right," I said.

"It is well," he replied.

My pastor, on the other hand, later told me that he was mortified when he looked up from the Sunday School lesson and found my former husband sitting right there in the audience. The topic for the day was 'Marital Abuse.' My pastor and I had a good laugh over that. But, in his usual fashion, my former spouse took it in stride, contributing to the interactive discussion the most and the loudest.

Unlike before, when we would sit together during the main service, we now sat on opposite sides of the church. This was not by design, though. By the time I finished up with another class I was in and walked into the main church, there were no more seats available on the side of the church where he happened to be sitting. Not that I would have sat right next to him, anyway. I could feel a few pairs of eyes boring curiously into my back when I walked into the sanctuary. This caused me no discomfort, though. This was my church, my home, and most people were used to this their 'crazy' sister. For whatever reason, most couples in my church don't sit together, anyway. For some, this is due to their varied church responsibilities which make it impossible for this to happen. For others without this predicament, I honestly don't get it, but 'different strokes for different folks,' as they say.

This is all still a bit weird, though, having him here, I thought to myself as I danced along to a catchy praise song the choir was belting out.

His visit also happened to coincide with my birthday, which was this past weekend. I had planned a party well in advance, having no inkling that he would be in town. Now that he was here, I couldn't exactly kick him out of the house for this one day. And being who he is, he felt no discomfort participating fully. He took more pictures at the party than anybody else, in fact, which irritated me ever so slightly. *What's he going to do with them?* I wondered, as I 'boogied' the afternoon away.

I felt sorry for those party guests who were friends with us as a married couple, and now felt a teeny bit awkward about having to relate with us as a divorced couple. I had to restrain myself from putting up a warning sign on the front door: *Sorry!! I didn't know he would be here!!!*

180

A particular couple that has apparently continued to root for us even though the divorce is now final were extremely excited to see him. The man ushered my children's father upstairs for a 'man to man' talk while the lady spontaneously gave me a second big hug in the kitchen, saying, "Give me another hug! Thank you, thank you – I had no idea he was in town!" I smiled back at her politely, thinking, *Thank you for what? The marriage is over, my dear sister. His presence here is not a sign that God is 'moving' or that we're getting back together*. They meant well, though, bless their hearts.

My point to my sister – who has since pronounced doom, convinced that my actions these past ten days have been unwise – and to anyone else who also (understandably) thinks I'm crazy, is that I'm new to this divorce thing. I'm just working things out a day at a time.

My children's father and I had a discussion about this whole weird divorce thing the night before he left.

"I have no major regrets about letting you stay here this time," I said, "but I don't know how I'll feel the next time. I'm taking this a day at a time. Next time, I might feel differently – who knows? I might start to feel really resentful about what I see as your presumptuousness. I don't want you to start getting complacent. We both just need to be prepared for anything. I realize that my letting you stay here now that we're divorced is really unconventional. It can be confusing to others and even to you, if I'm not careful."

"This whole divorce has been unconventional," he pointed out. "The fact that I didn't really fight you over the divorce in the first place was unconventional. The fact that we're not fighting now, is unconventional. People are just going to have to get used to it, and we're just going to have to consistently emphasize to them that we're no longer married until they get it."

What wisdom, I thought, staring at him for one fleeting, astonished moment. How come he didn't walk in this kind of wisdom and in this level of lucidity when his marriage was falling apart before his very eyes?

Oh well, I said to myself, brushing the thought off. *Spilt milk now.*

Spilt, evaporated, and vanished into thin air.

Divorce is complicated. But then, so are a lot of other things in life.

Great expectations

Hello, parent of an outstanding 8th grader!

You are receiving this email because we plan to give your son or daughter an award (sports, academic or character) at this year's Middle School Awards Ceremony, and we'd like you to be there to see it! The ceremony is on Friday, May 25th at 2 PM. We'll talk a little about why each award is given to that student, and we hope it will be encouraging to you and to your child. Please come if at all possible!

One other note: we like these to be a surprise for the students, so please don't mention it to your child beforehand.

*****

I was terribly excited to find the above email message from my son's school principal some months ago.

OMG, he's going to get an award in front of the whole school! I thought to myself. I gave myself several mental pats on the back. This was my reward for all the hours of yelling, scolding, threatening, taking away privileges, reiterating, and manipulating – all in a bid to keep my son on track. My 'Nigerian mother' tactics had finally paid off. This was my reward for all the hours I had spent helping out with homework after 'work-work,' until my schedule simply no longer permitted it.

I wondered what the prize would be for. Not sports because, for the first time last semester, he decided not to play a sport. It had to be academics. It just had to be. It would probably be for Math. So the money I spent each month on a Math tutor was really worth it! Or maybe not … maybe it was for English. That was more likely. His English teacher has always emphasized how well he writes. On a recent essay of his, she wrote: 'You are a good writer. Please pursue it and continue on this path. It is a pleasure to read your writing.' I put it up on the fridge (along with tons of other stuff) and it'll stay there until it disintegrates.

Wow – maybe my son would be a best-selling author some day! Or a scholar of some sort!

I could barely contain my excitement. What if the award was for character, though? Well … I suppose an award is an award, but I wasn't paying all that money in school fees for character, necessarily (sounds absolutely horrible, I know!). I mean, I suppose character development is always a welcome benefit one would hope for from a good school, but I teach character at home. Why pay that much for character when you can teach it yourself and save the money for college instead?

On the big day, I found myself a seat at the back of the auditorium since I would have to slip out right afterwards and rush all the way back across town again for a conference call at the office. My son sat between his two best friends on the other side of the room, totally oblivious to my presence and to the fact that he was getting an award.

My heart pounded in anticipation as they called out one student after the other, one award after the other. I hadn't expected this ceremony to take *forever*. I shifted impatiently in my seat as they called out *all* the sports awards and said a few words about each winner. Then came the academic awards. I watched and waited, holding my breath as they called out one student's name after the other … for one subject after the other … and as they called out my son's best friends one after the other … and as the academic awards session ended.

What a minute, I thought. *That only leaves … character.*

Okay, I suppose I can live with that, I thought, quickly swallowing my initial disappointment. They proceeded to call out one name after the other, along with one character trait after the other. *What other character trait could there possibly be*, I wondered.

As I waited impatiently to hear his name announced, I glanced over at my son's side of the room. I knew his two tight friends somewhat (as much as teenagers will let you know). Good kids (like mine) who had had several sleepovers at my house, eating a large dinner together, playing X-Box games through the night, talking and laughing in the dark until the early hours of the morning, and then playing some more the next day (with their unbathed, teenage selves), until it was time to go home. They were all so alike, it was uncanny – they even talked the same. After they spent some time at our house, I stopped bugging my son about mumbling all the time instead of actually talking. (Apparently, they all mumble and mutter at this age instead of enunciating properly.) How come they were focused enough to win an academic prize and mine wasn't? Well, when he got home, I would just have to point out to him that his best friends weren't any better than him and that I'd better see him up on that stage for an academic award next semester ... This 'Nigerian mama' train of thought was interrupted by the announcement of his name.

All I remember now is suddenly being filled to the brim with pride as my son walked confidently up to the stage, trying not to look fazed by what was to come (in eighth grade, you do have a reputation to protect, as he's explained to me before). I was absolutely bursting. I clapped until my hands hurt and totally forgot my previous thoughts.

The teachers decided to give my son an award for courage.

As one of the teachers explained, he's not afraid to express himself in class and through his school work – even if he does end up going slightly off on a tangent sometimes in a bid to be creative. A ripple of knowing laughter weaved through the teachers' section of the room. I joined them, nodding knowingly, and clapping harder. Yep, that's my son! "Get ready for this one," the teacher with the microphone said to a ninth grade teacher. "You're really going to enjoy having him in your class and reading the work he turns in. He's going to give you the ride of your life."

My son received his certificate and made his way back up to his seat. To his great surprise, there I was, standing right in his aisle behind his seat. His eyes lit up in spite of himself. I gave him a big hug and he actually (*shock*!) hugged me back, ignoring the stares of his fellow students. I suppose he lost some 'street cred' that day, but he didn't seem to mind this time – he was so shocked to see me that he forgot to be a teenager for a moment.

I totally forgot about the lecture I planned to give and decided to let my son just enjoy his moment in the spotlight.

"*I'm so proud of you,*" I whispered to him. And I was.

I thought about all my son had been through over the years, and how he had somehow, by the grace of God, pulled through. When his father started travelling, he was three. Back then, he would cry piteously into the phone, saying, "Come here, Daddy!" Wondering why he could hear his Daddy but couldn't see him. He cried less the next year, and even less the year after that. I noticed that he stopped crying completely when he was seven. How he has gone through life seeing his dad once a year or less, only God knows. How he made sense of his current life, only God knew. His teachers were more discerning than they realized. This was one courageous child and, boy, did he deserve that award!

Naija pikin no dey carry last, a-beg.

On my way back to the office, I pondered over how the love for a child is so unconditional. It's pure, pure *love*. Yeah, we have expectations for our children, but we can live with it if they aren't lived up to. There's just no greater love, I think, between humans. With people other than our children (including spouses), we usually tend to expect much more. At least I do.

Someone once said that 'expectation is the root of all heartache.' But what's the point of a relationship without expectations? Without them, from my perspective, all romantic relationships would be superficial and almost pointless. If I don't expect anything from you, and you have no expectations to meet … then is that really a relationship?

Consequences

D ivorce has consequences. Let no one tell you anything different.

But it's not because there's anything special about 'divorce.' Divorce in itself holds no unique powers. Getting divorced is an action or reaction. And any action (or inaction, for that matter) can potentially provoke a result – a consequence. Divorce has consequences. For this reason, when I was still married, a number of people wisely advised me to be very cautious about deciding to get divorced.

I want to say upfront that they were right.

Their account was as right as it was incomplete, though. What they neglected to mention is that marriage has negative consequences, too – an unhealthy marriage, I mean. That angle is usually completely overlooked. It's really not about two people staying together blindly, with no game plan for making things better.

Children are probably the number one reason why any parent considering divorce would hesitate and hesitate again over making this decision. I know it was a major reason for my lengthy, four-year period of making up my mind once and for all.

There are much-cited studies about the short- and long-term impacts of divorce on children. I remember watching *The Oprah Show*, many years ago, when, prompted by Judith Wallerstein's findings, Oprah did a segment on children of divorce who were now in their 40s. I watched with horror as grown, middle-aged men and women wept on the show. It simply ripped my heart out. I recall turning to my husband, who was watching along with me, and saying: "You know what? Let's make sure we don't get divorced, no matter what. If for nothing else than for the sake of this child (we only had one at the time), let's do whatever we can do stay together."

And, to be fair, we did. For a long time. But we did so blindly. We were visionless. We thought the miracle would stem from 'staying together,' and did not really ask ourselves what exactly that meant or could mean.

I compare my family now to my family then. I just want to say that my family now is not perfect. But it is better.

Not better because there haven't been challenges and hurdles to overcome – we have definitely had those – but better because we are wide awake and actively dealing with reality. In *Lies at the Altar: The Truth about Great Marriages*, Dr. Robin L. Smith says:

A lot of the time it just feels easier to curl up with a fantasy than to wake up to reality. But once you do wake up, it's hard to go back to sleep. And the longer you stay in a state of wakefulness, the better and more natural it feels.

In my family now – made up of my children and I – we have become much better at staying awake. Daily, we are staring our challenges in the eye and dealing with them with everything we've got, knocking them out one at a time. The child that actually remembers having two parents under the same roof has had a harder time of it, which is understandable. But even this child acknowledges that there is a lot to be grateful for, that at least one parent is here, and that no matter what, we will get through this together.

Although they have received less publicity, there are also studies concluding that "a 'healthy marriage' – and not just any marriage – is optimal for child well-being. Marriages that are violent or high conflict are certainly 'unhealthy,' for both children and adults."

I imagine fewer studies like this exist because, while a 'divorced' status is more cut and dried, identifying respondents who will admit to being in a 'bad' marriage must be fraught with challenges. But we all know people who, as children, wished or prayed that their parents would just get divorced already because of the turbulence in the home.

In church today, I was thinking about how my family's daily challenges have strengthened me, how much they have taught me, and how grateful each little victory along the way makes me feel. I reflected on how much my children have enriched my life. I cannot imagine what it would be like to be without them, as tough as it can be to be a single parent. I started to feel a bit selfish, actually, wondering how their dad coped with the reality of living without them, unable to watch them grow, and I thought back to see if *I* simply made it impossible for him to have them. Then I reminded myself that where I come from, children 'belong' to their father, so to speak, and any father that really wants the responsibility of taking care of his children barely has to raise a finger to make that happen legally. I was filled with a complex feeling that I get now and then – a combination of immense gratitude that my children's father did not fight to have them and a slight sense of bewilderment about why he did not.

I suppose it goes back to the fact that he knew their mother was 'capable' and that they would probably be better off in a stable, predictable home where their needs would be taken care of. I might have made the same decision if I were in his shoes. Why should I cause my children discomfort just to prove a point? Or maybe our cultural background makes it 'easier' for a man to sit back and wait patiently for his children to make the transition to adulthood, reasoning that they will always eventually seek out their father when they're independent. Whatever the reasons, my feeling of pure gratitude came back in the end. I'm just grateful that I have what I have.

I want to be careful not to sugarcoat things, though. The consequences of divorce can be horrible. This is true. The consequences of a bad marriage can be horrible. This is no less true. Let's not conveniently leave that part out simply because it doesn't quite fit with our philosophy of life.

Two different sets of consequences, but consequences just the same.

I took my pick.

Cutting Loose

I was searching for something in my purse without success one day. I searched three times and then decided to simply dump everything out. I came across an envelope and opened it to find – to my surprise – a stack of health insurance cards. They were old health insurance cards which had expired two years prior. Typically, I cut up my old insurance cards, so I wondered how these ones had escaped my attention for two good years. I also noticed that there were four of them, representing what used to be my family of four.

I stared at them and the memories of how I went from four cards two years ago to three cards today came back. I sifted through my emails to reconstruct the pathway that got me here, and to confirm the dates of each critical incident along the way.

This all started with a retirement account:

August 6: By this date, I have been separated from my then spouse for just under two years. I email my Human Resources department (HR) to find out if I can list my sisters, rather than my spouse, as the primary beneficiaries of my retirement account in case anything happens to me. I am informed that in order to do so, my spouse would have to waive his rights to being the primary beneficiary by signing the 'spousal consent' section of the retirement account form. I brace myself and prepare to have this difficult conversation with him. If anything happens to me, my sisters would know exactly what I want for my children (we're very similar when it comes to what we want for our children, what we think is best for children in general, and how we raise ours), and they're all really good with money management.

August 7 (I think): I discuss my plans (about the retirement account changes) with my spouse on the phone. He expresses displeasure. I sense that his displeasure is not about the money per se, but rather about the fact that my actions are a major indication that the relationship is over (access to a partner's finances can be such a deep sign of intimacy).

August 17: My spouse sends me an electronic copy of a signed 'spousal consent' section. I am very relieved. Relieved that I got it without any major hoopla, and almost proud of his attitude.

November 23 (the following year): I email HR to find out if it'll cost me less to have three members of my family (me and two children) covered by my health insurance rather than four (me, two children, and a husband). I'm told it'll cost me exactly the same amount, whether we're a party of three or a party of four. I chicken out from severing this tie with my spouse, reasoning that it's not costing me anything to just keep things as they are. What if he got sick where he was (God forbid.)? Wouldn't it be nice for him to be able to come over here and have his health taken care of? Why was I being 'wicked'? What did I stand to gain from this?

In the weeks to come, I wrestle with this issue. I come to the conclusion that I really shouldn't spend all this energy trying to take care of someone who didn't seem to be making any effort to take care of me or our children.

Still, I wait before making a move. I wait for another year.

December 8 (one year later): I email HR asking them to drop my spouse from my medical and dental coverage.

December 9: They reply saying they will process my request, and that this change will be effective as from January 1 the following year. They remind me that the amount deducted from my salary for this new arrangement will still be the same. I breathe in and out deeply, trying to push down the pangs of guilt.

April 15: It was about a year and a half later when I found the old insurance cards. The guilt is gone. It must have left long before now – I just haven't had an opportunity to think about this particular issue in a long time. And he has risen to the occasion. Although he's had his share of illnesses since I dropped him from my insurance, he has somehow sorted himself out.

The issue, though, was never that he wasn't capable of doing so. It was that he just didn't (or wouldn't). I would like to believe that, in the end, I helped both of us by making this tough decision.

I reached for the scissors on my desk, cut up the four cards into little pieces, and disposed of them in the bin.

Unrealistic

few months ago, we had a staff retreat at work. The hired facilitator took us through a soul-searching exercise. We were given a list of positive character traits and told to choose the top three that really defined us as individuals. I wrote my three down and now can't find them. But I do remember that one of the three I chose was 'dependable.'

I sat there feeling pleased (and perhaps a teeny bit smug) about my 'top three' which defined me completely and showed what a wonderful person I was. And then he showed us the potential flip side of each of the traits we had selected. Again, I don't remember what the others were, but the flip side of the word 'dependable' was the word … **'unrealistic.'**

I felt like I'd just been hit by a ton of bricks. For whatever reason, just seeing that solitary word had a profound, emotional effect on me. It literally knocked the wind out of my sails.

The facilitator's point was that every positive character trait can potentially turn into a particular negative trait if we're not careful and attentive.

I blinked my treacherous tears away.

I'm an unrealistic person.

Wow.

That was hard for me to swallow. Hard because I could see some truth in it. I blinked my tears away, thinking about how my older sisters always used to say I lived in 'my own little world' (thank goodness they've stopped saying this in recent times), and how I once saw an email my brother-in-law sent my then husband years ago, saying in frustration that I 'lived in a dream world.' It was in the early days of my ex-husband's business endeavors. His brother thought much of the business wasn't being handled properly and he marveled at the fact that I was supportive of the very idea of my husband being in business full-time in the first place – hence his comment. I was really hurt by that comment, but years later came to see the wisdom in it.

I suppose I do have an unrealistic side. I consider myself an extremely dependable person. I hate to let others down and will do everything within my power not to. Perhaps I have unrealistic expectations of others because I set such high standards for myself. Perhaps my views about some things are unrealistic and 'out of this world.' Maybe some of my wishes and dreams are unattainable. Maybe I spend too much time building castles in the air. There certainly is a side of me that loves to dream. But the thought that perhaps some of the things I hope for and dream about are not attainable in the first place brought tears to my eyes that day.

I occasionally ask myself which straw broke the camel's back for me: the increasing lack of participation in the marriage, or the infidelity. I lived with one for years until it became my norm. I guess I just couldn't live with the knowledge of *both*. I don't recall thinking I couldn't get past either of them; I was willing to work out the infidelity issues if I could be convinced that it wasn't going to be a lifestyle. It was the combination that killed me.

But then, what if it's simply unrealistic of me to expect that any African man can be faithful – Christian or not? What if the sort of socialization men receive makes it unthinkable that any of them would truly be able to rise above this pull of the flesh? And if that is indeed the case, then why did I bother getting a divorce? What gives me the idea that anyone else out there could be any different from my former husband? What if this is all just a dream world – one big hoax – and faith is just a strategic label that has no power to really change the heart?

Maybe you can't have it all. Or maybe (as they say) you can – just not all at the same time.

If I'm going to be in a marriage, though, then I want it all. And if that's unrealistic, then so be it. Rather than live without it in a marriage, I'll live without it alone.

If indeed I'm unrealistic, then I guess my God is, too. Unrealistic for having the following expectation:

"Drink water from your own cistern, running water from your own well. Should your springs overflow in the streets, your streams of water in the public squares? Let them be yours alone, never to be shared with strangers. May your fountain be blessed, and may you rejoice in the wife of your youth. A loving doe, a graceful deer – may her breasts satisfy you always, may you ever be intoxicated with her love. Why, my son, be intoxicated with another man's wife? Why embrace the bosom of a wayward woman? For your ways are in full view of the Lord, and he examines all your paths" (Proverbs 5: 15-21, NIV).

It wasn't always like this

I have a vivid memory of him carrying a bright pink bucket, a mop, several grocery bags (containing food, detergent, sponges, an electric kettle, and Lord knows what else). He had just returned from the grocery store about a mile or so away, looking like a hobo clutching all his worldly possessions. We had taken a leap of faith and moved to a new country that we knew absolutely nothing about, and this was our second night in our temporary apartment. I had just finished cooking our first meal in this little apartment, in this new country, and, unprompted by me, he wandered off to the store and brought back pretty much everything I needed to get us through the next couple of days. He had walked all the way there and back. I recall being filled, in that moment, with gratitude and relief to have a partner on this journey into the unknown.

I have another memory of him standing by the bed, on the opposite side from where I lay comfortably, still curled up and half asleep, across from our first baby. It was early in the morning and he was fully dressed for work. He picked up our son, who was about a month old and cradled him in his arms. "Are you happy yet?" he asked the baby, in all seriousness, and then paused as if actually waiting for an answer. "Are you happy to be a part of this family?"

And yet another memory of him at his son's very first doctor's appointment. The baby was tucked snugly into a little white sleep sack which the receptionist and nurses spent several minutes admiring. He carried his first child tenderly, proudly, possessively, barely taking his eyes off him. The receptionist and nurses whispered to each other about what a good dad he was while I silently agreed.

It's hard for my son to remember these things, as he was either too young, or they happened too long ago. He recently posed a series of questions that made me realize I have to remind him that things weren't always like this. There are some good memories and we must try not to forget that.

At one time, he was privileged to have a really good, committed father. He was the hands-on parent who would roughhouse with kids on the floor while I watched, amused, from a safe spot on the couch. He was the 'fun' one, who would let the children play on his laptop and the latest gadget he'd added to his collection, while I was Mrs. Killjoy, never failing to point out the possibility of expensive items getting damaged. He was patient and attentive toward them, while I was distracted by housework and work-work.

I just remember how he used to *try*.

Try to be there. And how he succeeded many, many times. As my sister once said, these memories are important for *me*, as they remind me that there were some good things, and that I wasn't completely crazy when I chose him (I'm just paraphrasing). But they're also important for me so that I can remind my children that it wasn't always like this. For a short time (much too short a time) in each of their lives, they caught a glimpse of what he has the potential to be. What caused the downward spiral to what I view as blatant indifference, we may never fully know for sure. But at least we can be grateful that we had *something*.

I had a wonderful father, personally. It breaks my heart that I can't give my children the same experience. But at least I can keep the memories of a few years alive for them.

It wasn't all bad. And so, today, I'm giving the guy a break. (I guess I'm feeling benevolent right now.)

Let's hear it for the boy. Let's hear it for the man.

Why I have no social life

"**D**o your children attend church with you?" he asked curiously.

"Of course, they do," I replied, bristling a little at the insinuation that they might not. I wondered for a second if my indignation made me come across as rude. He was a man of the cloth, after all, and really only trying to be sociable.

He stared me right in the eyes as if trying to see deep into my soul. He was clearly seeking for a word from the Lord where I was concerned.

After a minute, he said with conviction: "God will do it."

"Amen," I replied politely, after a moment's hesitation. I had no idea what exactly he was referring to, but I'm always open to being blessed in any area of my life, so I went along with it.

The church meeting had just ended and we were all spending a few minutes greeting one another before heading home. We hadn't met each other before, hence the curiosity. There were a number of children present, along with both of their parents. The absence of my own children from this meeting naturally made him wonder if they went to church with me at all. Given that I barely knew him, I didn't think it was worth it to explain that, just like all the men present, I had arrived straight from work. Unlike the men in attendance, I didn't have a partner at home to transport my children to the venue separately, and I lived too far away to pick them up myself and come all the way back before the session was over.

I ran into him again at a church meeting. He happened to be the speaker for the day. He delivered a good sermon and issued an altar call at the end for different categories of people. One of the last calls he made had to do with a troubled marriage.

"There is someone here: You're a married woman and you have had problems in your marriage. I want you to come out here, let me pray for you."

Hmmm ... I wonder who that could be, I said to myself, my eyes closed in prayer.

He repeated the call more forcefully. "There is a woman here who needs God to intervene in her marriage. God is a god of restoration; there is nothing impossible with Him. Come out, let me pray for you."

There was a hushed silence.

Well, that can't be me (I had already filed for divorce by this time and was satisfied with this decision).

"They have snatched your husband away from you and you don't want to pray. Come out here, let us pray for you," the pastor repeated with a hint of irritation.

Did he really go there? I asked myself in disbelief. *If everyone is waiting for me to walk out to the front of the church, they're wasting their time. Am I the only one with marital issues? Besides, nobody 'snatched' my husband from me.*

My former marital challenges understandably led some to the conclusion that my husband was taken away while I stood there, wringing my hands and watching helplessly. The idea that a Nigerian, Christian woman could proactively choose my current path is almost inconceivable – much too unusual for most people to imagine that I even had a choice.

Apart from the fact that it's inaccurate, I simply didn't like this portrait of myself which I presumed was being painted by others. I didn't like this idea, either, that I (or whoever else) only 'deserved' prayer if I walked out to the front of the church. For whose benefit, I wondered? Was this an absolute requirement from God, or was this more about personal ego on the part of humans? I wondered if those around me (who might have expected me to obediently identify myself) were secretly offended by my stubbornness.

Maybe I was just being unnecessarily sensitive.

I know my views aren't exactly popular, and I'm sorry (sincerely) if I come across as irreverent or unspiritual. I'm very sensitive to the reality that I may come across this way and so I try to make things easier for everybody. As much as I *love* to relate with people, I now subconsciously steer away from too much social interaction. I steer away from married women to spare them the discomfort of having to decide whether to befriend me or not. I do this with a full understanding of what it's like to be married and have your husband tell you he's uncomfortable with your friendship with a particular girlfriend. Rather than have this situation arise, I maintain a noticeable distance, while being polite and friendly.

That way, anyone that actually wants to be a friend of mine has to deliberately seek me out, understanding what they're getting into. That way, there are no hard feelings if I'm not sought after – and, hopefully, no feelings of guilt on the part of others for (understandably) deciding not to seek me out. That way, I avoid potential accusations (from husbands) of attempting to negatively influence their wives (something that's typical of my people), just because we happen to be having a conversation, and accusations from wives of being interested in their husbands.

My divorce aside, I'm also cognizant of the fact that I live a very different life from most of the married women I am acquainted with – and there is absolutely nothing I can do about it. While they are in this country as a consequence of their husbands' jobs, I happen to be here because of mine. I therefore have to work as hard as any of their spouses (if not harder), leaving me with much less time than I would have had, had I accompanied my husband to this post instead. The limited amount of time that I have (and my absence from social circles as a result) could give others the impression that I'm aloof or even arrogant. Nothing could be further from the truth, though. I in fact think about their lives with a tinge of envy sometimes, wishing I had the luxury of being a 'kept' woman, too – and I sometimes see a flash of envy in their eyes as well, when they look at me, imagining that I lead a glamorous life as an 'independent career woman.' The grass always looks greener on the other side, I suppose.

I guess I'm fortunate that I've never been what you could call a social butterfly. I've always had 'hermit-like' tendencies, so these new adjustments to my life aren't really that much of an adjustment. This doesn't mean that I'm not absolutely crazy about people, though. My relationships have always been few because my relationships have always been deep. I pour my soul into them. I give my all and don't hold back. And that's why when I'm 'done,' I'm really done. I only get 'done' because after giving all that I have, all that I am, I honestly have nothing left to give. I have few relationships because I don't know how to do relationships superficially. Maybe that's not such a good thing. Deep relationships require energy, and there's only so much energy to go round.

But what happens to women that are wired totally differently from the way I am? Divorced, African, Christian women that also happen to be extroverted? Women that really crave social interaction but can't get it because of all the barriers I've mentioned and more? Where do we talk about this? When something like this happens, where do you go?

Where do you turn to when the world you gave your life to is suddenly no longer tailored for people like you?

Happens to the best of us

Divorce can and does happen to the best of us sometimes. We ask ourselves why divorce 'happened' to us. And we're not the only ones; other people want to know why, too.

We're used to having a reason for everything, to being able to explain everything away. There's got to be some tangible reason why you couldn't hold it together. After all, the scripture says, 'The wise woman builds her house, but with her own hands the foolish one tears hers down (Proverbs 14: 1, NIV).' Forget the fact that this verse needs to be understood within some sort of context. I've met many women whose husbands clearly did the 'tearing down,' and yet who use this verse to absolve the erring party from all responsibility. If your marriage didn't last, the first thought is often that it must have had everything to do with *you*.

When concerned Christians learn about my divorce, they want a concrete reason why this happened to 'someone like me.' I understand where they are coming from and actually look at their search for that one reason as a compliment, in a way. I don't need anyone to tell me what a gem I am. It's natural for anyone to wonder why a gem wouldn't be treated like a gem. What did you do to make someone else treat you like less than what you're supposed to be? It must be that the person concerned discovered some sort of deficiency in the gem to make him/her appreciate it less. In a roundabout sort of way, sometimes people try to find out *why*. What is it about you that's not immediately obvious?

'Are you sure you were cooking for the man?' It's fascinating to me to see how shocked people are to find out what a good cook I am (if I may say so myself!). Seriously – visitors to my house usually leave a bit stunned. I didn't realize until fairly recently that so many people assumed that I (a Nigerian woman at the age of 40) either couldn't cook at all, or couldn't cook 'real' Nigerian food.

With the food issue settled, next comes the sex issue. 'Are you sure you were not in the habit of refusing to have sex with your husband?'

If you must know: no, I am not frigid, and I can count the number of times I refused to have sex when I had a husband. Twice to be exact – once when I was ill, and another time when I was upset over an unresolved issue and the idea of 'make-up' sex didn't appeal to me.

'So, what was the problem, then?'

My guess is as good as yours. Sometimes, you can't explain why things began to unravel. And my lack of a concrete explanation takes nothing away from the fact that I'm a wonderful person. I'm an absolute gem. I knew it then and I know it now. If I were not me, I'd want to be my friend.

I suppose that, in a way, this overly-favorable opinion of myself accounts for my indignation over my former husband's passivity, during the time when (in my opinion) action was sorely needed. *Did he not realize what a gem he was losing? Did he not realize his wife was one in a million?*

It's possible that he did, but that he just knew me well enough to know that I'm pretty careful with my words and I only say what I mean – and if I said it was over, then I meant it. And if I meant it, there was probably no need trying to get me to change my mind. Who knows?

At the last family meeting convened to try and salvage the marriage, he said publicly: "I understand why she's doing what she's doing. I've done a lot of things. I've done a lot of things that she doesn't even know about. If I were her, I would divorce me, too."

There was a shocked silence from everyone present.

I wondered what God had saved me from. I *still* wonder what God saved me from.

In everything, we are to give thanks.

Even in this, Lord?

Yes, even in this.

Sometimes, a sense of gratitude is the appropriate response toward the demise of a marriage – even a Christian one.

'I hate divorce' ... says the Lord

"'I hate divorce," says the Lord ..."' (Malachi 2:16, NIV).

Yep, the Lord Himself said it. God hates divorce. And if I'm a Christian and I want to please Him, logically, I should hate divorce and the people and paraphernalia associated with it, too, right?

Not so fast.

It is tempting (not to mention, convenient) to fixate on this sentence while ignoring the entire verse from which it has been extracted, and the chapter that gave rise to this striking declaration. As a divorced Christian, however, I am naturally curious about *why* God made this statement. My divorce demands that I investigate this at least a little further.

I will not reproduce the entire chapter here, but it would be irresponsible of me not to at least review a few verses in order to provide more context. Fortunately, in this day and age, there are many different versions of the Bible to choose from and to compare with each other in order to have a balanced perspective on any issue. I have chosen to review Malachi 2:11-16 in the New Living Translation. It states the following:

Judah has been unfaithful, and a detestable thing has been done in Israel and in Jerusalem. The men of Judah have defiled the Lord*'s beloved sanctuary by marrying women who worship idols. May the* Lord *cut off from the nation of Israel every last man who has done this and yet brings an offering to the* Lord *of Heaven's Armies.*

Here is another thing you do. You cover the Lord*'s altar with tears, weeping and groaning because he pays no attention to your offerings and doesn't accept them with pleasure. You cry out, "Why doesn't the* Lord *accept my worship?" I'll tell you why! Because the* Lord *witnessed the vows you and your wife made when you were young. But you have been unfaithful to her, though she remained your faithful partner, the wife of your marriage vows.*

Didn't the Lord *make you one with your wife? In body and spirit you are his. And what does he want? Godly children from your union. So guard your heart; remain loyal to the wife of your youth. "For I hate divorce!" says the* Lord, *the God of Israel. "To divorce your wife is to overwhelm her with cruelty," says the* Lord *of Heaven's Armies. "So guard your heart; do not be unfaithful to your wife."*

Verse 16 in particular is worth examining more closely, given the popularity of its first sentence. Here it is, in six different versions of the Bible:

"I hate divorce," says the Lord God of Israel. "I hate it when one of you does such a cruel thing to his wife. Make sure that

211

you do not break your promise to be faithful to your wife." (Good News Translation)

For the Lord, the God of Israel, saith that he hateth putting away: for one covereth violence with his garment, saith the Lord of hosts: therefore take heed to your spirit, that ye deal not treacherously. (KJV)

The Lord God of Israel says, "I hate divorce. And I hate people who do cruel things as easily as they put on clothes," says the Lord All-Powerful. So be careful. And do not break your trust. (New Century Version)

For the Lord, the God of Israel, says he hates divorce and cruel men. Therefore, control your passions—let there be no divorcing of your wives. (The Living Bible)

"I hate divorce," says the God of Israel. God-of-the-Angel-Armies says, "I hate the violent dismembering of the 'one flesh' of marriage." So watch yourselves. Don't let your guard down. Don't cheat. (The Message)

"I hate divorce," says the Lord God of Israel, "and I hate a man's covering himself with violence as well as with his garment," says the Lord Almighty. So guard yourself in your spirit, and do not break faith. (New International Version).

To me, the pattern that emerges from various translations of this verse is as clear as the connotation: God hates divorce for the devastation it causes. God does not hate divorced people. God implored men to be faithful to their wives because unfaithfulness signified a broken covenant, and could lead to divorce and devastation. God hates divorce because of what it often *symbolizes*: A breach of trust. A flippant attitude toward the notion of self-control. A means of deliberately meting out cruelty in an era when being unmarried and female meant being unprotected.

The truth is that the second chapter of Malachi isn't really about divorce. It's about unfaithfulness (in our spiritual marriage to God and in our earthly marriages to one another) which God describes as 'detestable.' Divorce is merely one of its by-products.

This explains the why the well-known sentence, 'I hate divorce,' is conjoined to words such as 'so,' and 'therefore':

'I hate divorce ... therefore take heed to your spirit, that ye deal not treacherously.'

'I hate divorce …. So be careful. And do not break your trust.'

It's interesting to me that in this particular passage, despite His hatred for divorce, God doesn't necessarily use this opportunity to ask that his interlocutors refrain from getting divorced. Rather, He uses it to demand that they be faithful and upright. Clearly, this is because such virtues can help keep divorce at bay. The question then becomes: What does God really hate in the context of this Scripture? Is it divorce in itself (an end-product), or behaviors that can lead to it?

God's concern for wives is also evident from this passage. My reading of it is that He was concerned about the severely disadvantaged position that divorce placed a woman in during that era. He therefore regarded divorce as a cruel, violent, selfish act against such women – particularly since the verses imply that men were divorcing their wives just so they could cavort with various women.

I believe God knows that faithfulness can be a struggle sometimes, though. It doesn't happen without determination or without a fight. Which is why He urges us (in the different translations) to do exactly that: *fight*. Don't break your promise. Don't be treacherous. Control your passions. Watch yourself. Don't let your guard down. Don't cheat. Be careful. Don't break your trust. Do not be unfaithful to your spouse.

Yes, God hates divorce, and, being divorced myself, I understand exactly why.

Not my daughter

"**H**ow do you think you'll feel – at the age of 40 – living as a divorced woman for the rest of your life?"

Ordinarily, I would have found this an interesting question. But it came from my spouse several months before our divorce came through and so, naturally, I felt insulted by it while also understanding where it was coming from. It's not uncommon for me to experience these weird, twin emotions of resentment and sympathy all at once.

I understood that this question really represented his own fears, disguised and packaged to look like mine.

Don't try to make your fears mine, I wanted to say.

Fear is a very personal thing and, under normal circumstances, no one can choose or name the fear of another. I don't need anyone to tell me what to be afraid of.

It was on the tip of my tongue to retort that being married until the age of 40 hadn't been such a picnic, either. That would've made my flesh feel really good, but, as usual, I restrained myself and came back at him with silence, leaving it up to him to try and figure out what my silence meant.

I also sensed that the question was a last ditch attempt at trying to get me to change my mind, even if it meant manipulating me into doing so. I wondered why anyone would want that – that is, why anyone would want a spouse that stayed with them only because they were 'tricked' into it, or only for the sake of keeping up appearances. I wondered why he didn't want more than that out of a marriage, out of life.

If he was just trying to get me to change my mind, then I have to admit it was a smart move – this attempt to play into the typical fears of women. Although I bristled at the suggestion that *I* would remain alone for the rest of my life (rather than *him*), truth be told, his strategy of drawing my attention to this sensitive area was actually brilliant. Ever before this book became a book, it was a blog. At that time, there were a certain proportion of women that discovered the blog purely by chance. It is telling that the majority of women in this category were browsing the internet in search of effective prayers against 'strange women,' or in search of strategies for handling running into 'The Other Woman.'

I was saddened that this was the case. I was saddened by the reality that (for many good reasons) we have been obligated to make this our battle. That in addition to waging war against the potential 'strange woman,' if she ends up being part of our lives anyway, we then have to 'fortify' ourselves to handle running into her.

Maybe I'm just way too jaded, but I refuse to pray this type of prayer. I'm not recommending that anyone else follow suit.

I believe you should do whatever works for you within the context of godliness. For me personally, though, I reject this subtle notion that all husbands are 'bewitched' (and therefore simply incapable of taming their penises) – while their wives are not. When the Bible talks about there being 'neither Jew nor Gentile, slave nor free,' going further to add: 'nor is there male and female' (Galatians 3: 28, NIV), I really believe it.

I do not believe that men will have special concessions on Judgment Day simply because they are men and can't help themselves. I do not deny that socialization is a powerful thing, but if our predicament is brought about by socialization, then let's say so, and stop trying to spiritualize that which is merely social – and let's deal with it as a social issue instead of fixating on expending spiritual energy.

This is not the kind of world that I want to hand down to my daughter. I want a very different world for her. But perhaps that's just wishful thinking. And if so, then I *thank God* my daughter is nothing like me. Unlike me, she has always been very clear in her own mind about what she wants, and she wants what she wants without embarrassment or apology. She is far from a 'people pleaser,' and her expectations are crystal clear. This sort of attitude is sure to keep her on a less complicated path than I have trod.

If the world won't change, then I suppose the people in it have to.

Waiting on the world

If this isn't the sort of world I want for my daughter, it's not the sort of world I want for my son, either. This world in which good male role models are rare, and in which the expectations for men get lower by the generation – and, as a consequence, a world in which my son may be tempted to aspire for less. This world in which men's needs and vulnerabilities are overlooked in order not to tamper with the veneer of their 'manliness.' This word in which 'manliness' can hold a man captive, even as it gives the appearance of offering him enviable advantages.

My son introduced me to John Mayer about 3 months ago. He'd been bugging me to listen to this one song for a couple of weeks – one of his favorites. (I had heard of John Mayer, but couldn't really tell you at that time anything about his songs.) I finally found some time and he played it for me. I then realized I'd heard the song quite a few times and actually really liked it, but just didn't know any of the words. I finally took the time to listen. In his riveting song, *Waiting on the World to Change* (for anyone else who lives under a rock like me and doesn't know this already), John Mayer describes the helplessness of humanity in the face of this world's challenges. We feel so helpless that we resign ourselves to *waiting*. Waiting on the world to change.

The song reminded me of being stuck in a bad marriage and waiting, hoping something outside of the marriage would one day show up and make things better.

Leaving a 'bad' marriage isn't necessarily a solution. It's not necessarily the magic bullet. But what it can do is open the door for you to eventually find or discover the actual 'magic.'

Even then, the 'magic' isn't offered on a silver platter. You need the gumption to get up and *walk* through that open door.

Staying, in itself, isn't the magic bullet, either. I know because I stayed, too – for 14 years. But I stayed passively, and that was a mistake. I have learned that, even in staying, one must take action to create the life that one wants.

In *Happily Ever After Divorce: Notes on a Joyful Journey*, Jessica Bram writes: 'When you ... become part of a couple, there's gain, but also loss.' I think this is true whether you're part of a couple, whether you're single, divorced, or separated. There's something to gain from each of these statuses, and every one of them can also be associated with something that can't quite be defined as 'gain.'

The point is: the grass is not necessarily greener on the other side. As the saying goes, it's greenest where you water it. And that's what I'm determined to do: water my own grass. Because it's not about the grass, necessarily. It's about what's done to or with the grass.

In trying to water my own grass, I guess I'm making a statement that change (in my world and in yours) starts with *me*. We're waiting on our world to change, but maybe our world is waiting on *us*.

'For I consider that the sufferings of this present time (this present life) are not worth being compared with the glory that is about to be revealed to us and in us and for us and conferred on us! For [even the whole] creation (all nature) waits expectantly and longs earnestly for God's sons [and daughters – my addition] to be made known.' (Romans 8: 18-19, Amplified Bible)

What's in a name?

"**D**o you plan to go back to your maiden name?" someone asked, sometime before my divorce was final.

I hesitated for a minute.

I hadn't thought about my name, frankly.

When I was much younger, I remember thinking about just how difficult it would be for me to give up my maiden name. It sounded 'just right' along with my first name, I always thought. Why would I want to mess that up? Later on, in my twenties, the idea of changing my name seemed more exciting and like something to look forward to – a testament to my complete trust in this new person whom my life would forever revolve around.

When marriage time came around, I recall being pleased that my new name wasn't so completely different from my maiden name. I quite liked the sound of it, actually.

Professionally, I have always used my married name, which means that this is the name that pretty much everyone in my world knows me by. Interestingly (although no one would ever know it), I never actually changed my maiden name officially. My full maiden name is still on every official document I own – from passports and bank accounts, to pay slips and driver's licenses.

One of my sisters always figured she would have a hyphenated name when she got married – and she did. Another sister took a day off from work to go around town and fill out all the necessary forms to ensure her married name was changed officially. I recall admiring her energy at the time.

I'm searching myself as I write this to figure out if there was some subconscious reason why I didn't change my name officially. I honestly don't think so, though. At the time, I figured that since email communication was increasingly important (and really 'defined' you, in a sense), and I used my married name on all my email accounts, my name was 'changed' without all the stress of visiting numerous offices to formalize it. I only introduced myself by my married name, so no one ever called me anything else. If I didn't tell you I hadn't changed it, you would never know. My former spouse never raised it, either. Everyone called me by his name, and if getting some mail with my maiden name on it bothered him, he never mentioned it.

With the marriage over, I sometimes wish going back to my maiden name were an uncomplicated process. I know that a lot of divorced women stick with their married names in order not to have a different surname from their children. I appreciate this need to preserve order, but don't personally think I'd feel terribly uncomfortable using a different surname from my children. For me, it's more about avoiding professional confusion. It would be confusing (for others) at this stage to change my name professionally, and so the idea is not appealing at this time for that particular purpose.

For some other purposes, though, I find the idea of reverting back to my maiden name quite attractive. Maybe I should have hyphenated it to begin with, or used it as my middle name. That way, 'shaking off' my married name would have been much easier. I now marvel, in fact, that I was ready to give it up so quickly. There's a lot about my maiden name to be proud of, and I now wonder that I didn't hesitate even a teeny bit to have no one call me by it ever again.

Good thing that as long as we know who we are, we're always what or who we are, regardless of what anyone else calls us.

What d'you do for sex?

One emotion that the news of my divorce sometimes invokes in people is pity. Several Christians I know have been concerned about my being 'too young' to be a divorcée.

"You're too young to be on your own," some say, pityingly.

"How are you going to manage completely on your own?" others ask, not referring to my financial situation.

A couple of bold, Christian friends have come right out and said what others have been too uncomfortable to say. They have told me point blank that they're concerned about my sexual needs.

I've been really touched by this. I have some *really* good friends.

Sex really is a key consideration, and I suppose the reality of having no sex life is partly behind the solemn warnings I've gotten from some Christians who do not believe in re-marriage after divorce, and who wonder how one can possibly manage leading a sexless life when still in one's 'prime.' For many, the sex question is important enough for one to re-consider a divorce decision.

Indeed, what *does* a Christian woman do about sex, once divorced? And why wasn't sex (or the possibility of never having any ever again) enough reason to keep me married?

I have several answers to these important questions. The one that immediately comes to mind is that I've never been the sort of person to have sex with just anybody. Sex, for me, has to be meaningful. I suppose this is why, although I had romantic relationships with the opposite sex prior to marriage, the privilege of actually having sex with me was reserved for the man I was going to marry.

When the marriage was hanging on its last thread due to all that I discovered, I realized that the sex was no longer meaningful. As one person put it: 'That's why adultery is called adultery – because it "adulterates," which literally means to make something poorer in quality by adding another substance.' Standing back from my 'adulterated' marriage, I realized I could never bring myself to have sex with my spouse again. I no longer knew who he was. I understood that he was only human, fallible like the rest of us. But the lack of acknowledgment, the lack of ownership of the damage caused, was not something that I expected from the person I thought I knew. I wondered who this stranger was in the house. I knew then that the sex was over. Like I said, I don't sleep with just anybody.

Now that I'm no longer married, I try to maintain a realistic perspective about sex. Sex is great, but I try to avoid romanticizing it. I tell myself the truth about sex (as far as I can remember):

1. Sometimes, you're in the mood for it, and sometimes, you're not.

2. When I was married and could legitimately have sex, there were times that I didn't really want to.
3. If I asked most married couples how often they have sex in a week (or even in a month), if they're truthful, I may find that they're not having much more sex than me.
4. Unmarried Christians aren't the only ones that have to do without sex. So do the married, sometimes: when the relationship simply isn't working out and this has negatively impacted sexual desire; when one's spouse is ill and simply not up to it; when one's partner is out of town; when sleeping arrangements have to be modified temporarily for various reasons (visitors from out of town, sick children that want to sleep with Mommy and Daddy, etc.) ...
5. Sex is just like any other thing I can't have right now. Like chocolate cake. It would be great to have some, but once I realize I *can* have some, and then *do* have some ... it eventually loses its appeal.
6. During my marriage, I hardly ever saw my spouse, anyway. So my current, sexless life really isn't a whole lot different.

The bottom line, though, is that as a married Christian, sex (with your spouse) is at least an option. So, when it's no longer an option, what recourse do you have?

I read somewhere that exercise is beneficial in this regard. As sex is (among other things) a form of exercise, it makes sense to me that regular exercise would make a good (if only partial) replacement.

I've also come to see my extremely busy life as a gift. I honestly lead such a busy life now, that I sometimes marvel at how I ever managed to fit a husband and the regular demands of marriage into my schedule. (Then again, as my then husband was hardly ever present, perhaps that explains it!)

Finally, I find that, at the end of the day, sex is about fulfillment. We all need to feel fulfilled, and there are many ways to get there. I find that reading fulfills me. So does writing. So does spending time with my children when I don't have distracting deadlines. So does helping people in need. So does spending time with my friends. So does cooking splendid meals for others. So does encouraging others.

Being excited about my life, finding things that excite me and make me grateful for being alive, being present for my life, not missing the recital of my own life, dreaming and planning for my children's future and for my own … these are examples of important things that overshadow many other things I might be missing – including sex.

Although it seems like the married 'have it all' when it comes to the sex question, I remind myself that at least I have something to look forward to, if I ever do decide to re-marry. And expectation in itself, anticipation in itself, is a blessing.

'African, Christian, and Divorced?'

I had an interesting, cross-country conversation with an old friend of mine. Interesting because the conversation brought up a lot of questions that I'm sure other African Christians would like to ask a Christian woman in my position. We hadn't talked in a while and so she had only just found out about my divorce by taking a cursory look at excerpts from this book back when it was a blog. She called me soon afterwards. We caught up on the events that had occurred in each other's lives over the previous year or more, while she did her housework. She was cleaning her bathroom as we spoke.

"Some Christians will wonder why you actually had to get a divorce – why you didn't just stay separated. How would you respond to that?" she asked, in the tone of a CNN reporter, scrubbing away at her bathtub.

Reading between the lines, I knew she was really asking this question for her own benefit, trying to figure out how I could possibly make sense of my Christianity as a divorced person who spent her Christian life being warned against divorce.

I don't know how to be a non-Christian divorcée. I became a Christian a lifetime ago – at age 14. Even if I did believe that my getting divorced was a sin (which I don't), I wouldn't know how to even begin to shed my Christian skin. I don't know how not to be what I am. I don't know how not to be both – i.e., a Christian and a no-longer-married woman.

Out of curiosity, I asked her if she believed I was going to hell because I got divorced, hoping to myself as I asked that the question was inoffensive.

"No," she said without hesitation.

I honestly don't think she said this to try and be polite. I could almost hear, though, over the phone, an audible clash between this opinion and her long-standing belief that divorce has always got to be a sin.

"So you're writing about sex, too, huh – you Christian woman, you?" She chided half-jokingly, half-seriously, switching to a 'lighter' topic.

"Absolutely," I quipped. "What's un-Christian about it?"

We both have five children between us, I thought to myself, mentally calculating. This (usually) doesn't happen without a fair amount of sex – not even for anointed Christians.

Squish, squish, squish, her scrubbing brush went over the phone.

"So, what exactly do you say about it?"

"Read the book," I responded.

"I will, but just tell me why you had to write about it."

"Because I think it's interesting how we forget that your sexuality doesn't disappear just because you got divorced – or because you're widowed, for that matter. I think it's interesting how we don't address this issue. I'm intrigued by how people often think the solution is to give a no-longer-married woman more and more church responsibilities to ensure she's sufficiently 'distracted' by the things of God, hoping that's the panacea, rather than help her deal with her sexuality in practical ways that glorify God; how there's this assumption that sexuality is only an issue for young, unmarried people, rather than for *all* people – including married people."

I recall that several well-meaning people thought it would be a great idea for me to enroll in Bible School, once they learned about my new status. I have nothing against Bible School, but the idea of going there myself has never been appealing. That's actually one of the last things I would like to do. Divorce has not changed this. I don't need to be distracted or in denial. I need to deal. I *want* to deal.

"So, how do you explain how it all came to this? I mean, the divorce." *Squish, squish, squish*, went the scrubbing brush in the background.

Again, I read between the lines. "Do you mean how I make sense of the fact that this happened to me, even though I'm a Christian that's supposed to be abundantly 'blessed'?"

"Yes," she said.

"READ THE BOOK," I said.

"You mean you talk about that, too?"

"Yep."

"Okay, but just tell me what you say about it, in a nutshell."

"What I hope the book conveys is that there are no easy answers to this question. I hope I can convey the fact that divorce is much more complex than I ever would have known had I not experienced it myself. I say that although I realize people will always assume (at least initially) that, as a divorced woman, I was 'abandoned,' the divorce was actually my making. And at the same time, it wasn't – at least not completely. This didn't just 'happen to me' in the way that we tend to presume. In a sense, it happened to me while I also 'made it happen.' I think it's interesting that this question does not come up while you're in a bad marriage. No one asks how this could have happened to you. As long as you're married, nothing can possibly be amiss. The alarm begins and the questions arise when you're no longer in the marriage. To me, that's much too late."

I'm reminded here of a chilling comment I found in response to a post on marriage therapist Susan Berger's website, *About Affairs*. The thought-provoking comment made my heart bleed. The commenter was the daughter of a minister/pastor and a stay-at-home mother who had what externally seemed like the 'perfect' marriage. There was absolutely no infidelity involved in the relationship – in fact, the commenter remarks that the marriage was characterized by 'perfect fidelity.' However, as she describes it:

> They "stuck it out" for 37 years before my Dad died ... And yet, [their] marriage was ... a nightmare ... and it was excruciating to watch them interact in my Dad's final years. I won't go into detail, but I found this to be perhaps the most disillusioning

experience of my life. Despite their best efforts, their marriage was NOT a vehicle for personal growth and development. Their characters did NOT improve with time. There was NO mellowing, no growing wiser with age. Somehow, they managed not to do anything "wrong," but they missed out on the opportunity to do some important things right. But they clung to the assurance they they'd lived "right," not betrayed each other, stuck to their commitment, etc. And I guess I found that to be a lie, and as much of a deceit, to themselves, to each other, and to their children, as an affair. There are many ways that life can go "off the rails," and one of them is sticking to course at all costs.

I read this comment again this morning, after not having looked at it in a while. I find that I still reel over the combination of eloquence, beauty, pain, and loss of innocence that the post represents. It gives me pause that this was written, not from the perspective of a no-longer-married woman such as myself, but from that of a child who watched a bad marriage happen between two Christian parents. I'm saddened for the parents of this child, who must have meant well and most likely did the best they could, within the realm of knowledge available to them. I'm saddened about the total waste of nearly four decades of life – ironically, all in a sincere bid to please God. I'm saddened for the children, who were crying out for parents that were 'real,' not perfect. In reading the anonymous comment again today, I'm reminded of the hauntingly beautiful scripture that says, '[T]he letter killeth, but the spirit giveth life' (II Corinthians 3: 6).

When exactly does divorce begin? This is a deep question which I have agonized over in my own life. Does it begin when you receive your final divorce decree, or does it begin way before that? Sort of like adultery. We like to imagine it begins when the physical deed is done, but we know it begins in the heart, way before anyone else can see anything is amiss. Sort of like emotional affairs, which some erroneously see as harmless. Every woman knows that emotional affairs (where there may be no physical touching at all) are so much more painful than affairs that are purely physical. If you decide to let someone else touch your body, that's one thing, but to let them touch your *heart* takes the sense of betrayal to a whole other level.

I tell my friend that divorce is a complicated issue.

"Hmm! 'African, Christian, and Divorced,' eh? What is this book really about?" she said accusingly, at the very beginning of our conversation, referring to the title of this chapter.

I laughed in amusement. At least she was open about her own struggle to make sense of the new divorced, me. I'm still the same person, but I can't pretend to be married, when I'm not.

"Before, *nko*?" I replied. "Should I have said 'African, Moslem, and Just Got Married'?"

We both laughed at the absurdity of that idea.

I understood that her *real* questions, throughout this conversation – the questions she *really* meant to ask, but didn't, for fear of sounding insensitive, were: *Are you still the Christian I used to know? Can you really be divorced and still a genuine Christian? Help me understand this new thing that my friendship with you has forced me to confront.*

These are questions that I personally don't struggle with, frankly. I feel quite comfortable leaving the validation of my Christianity to God. In the end, He will be the Judge, anyway. The judgments of women and men, though understandable, are neither here nor there, in the grand scheme of things. One day, I will be judged by the only wise and righteous Judge. On that day, I will receive the only judgment that matters.

Am I still really a Christian? I tell my youth class that Christianity is, among other things, an issue of identity.

But I didn't know you were Nigerian – you don't act like a Nigerian!

If I had a dollar for every time I've met someone that has said I don't 'act' or 'sound' or 'look' or 'seem' Nigerian, I'd have to quit my day job because I'd be a millionaire by now. While it's interesting that people may perceive me as not 'seeming' to be something, it does nothing to change who and what I am – unless, of course, I let it.

"So have you written about me in the book?" my friend asked, in conclusion.

"Come to think of it, I have."

"Really? What did you say?"

"READ THE BOOK!!!"

"Stop shouting – make sure you write about me."

"Don't worry, I will."

On re-marriage

I often get asked if I will ever get married again. My answer to this question is that I have no idea. Sometimes I think there's a 50-50 chance that this could happen, and other times, I think the chances are zero.

I do not know if I can truly trust again, or if I even *want* to, knowing what can happen. Why would I want to put myself in a position to potentially go through something like this a second time? And this saddens me because I always prided myself as being 'marriage/wife material.' It saddens me that the experiences leading up to my divorce seem to have radically altered my very essence. This means that I'm suddenly no longer the same person anymore and I have to get to know who this new person is for myself before I even consider sharing her with anyone else. I really *liked* who I used to be. Or at least my personal notion of who I was back then. I suppose I could get to like who I am now much better (since she's much smarter) but I don't know her well enough yet.

When I was married, marriage, for me, was largely about giving. I am not sure that I want to give that much ever again, or to make any one person so central to my very existence. Having done it before, I now find the idea absolutely terrifying.

I would also have to learn how to demand and how to receive, and those would be new skills for me. I'm not sure that this 'old dog' (terribly inappropriate term, I know) wants to learn 'new tricks' at this age.

To further complicate matters, I'm an 'all or nothing' sort of person. (Remember Daouda Dieng in Mariama Ba's *So Long a Letter*? I loved that guy! 'All or nothing.') I'm beginning to think that this is a rather extreme way to be. Perhaps I need to exist within more of a happy medium between the two (i.e., 'all' or 'nothing'). But how do you switch from being an idealist all your life to being a cynic all of the sudden? This, too, would be a brand new skill that I'm not sure I really want to acquire.

And who wants to go through the trouble of having to blend a family (which would be a likely reality, getting re-married at this stage in life)? Or of not knowing whether someone will love my children, or whether my children would like *them*? Or whether *their* children would like *me* – or whether *I* would like *them*? Goodness! Far too much trouble.

The good thing is that (surprisingly, wondrously) my primary considerations here have nothing to do with the real possibility of being alone for a VERY long time (a very valid fear). My primary considerations are about whether re-marriage would be *a good deal* for me and my children. (I'm REALLY pleased that I've grown up at least somewhat.)

So there you have it. I have no idea. I'm open to being surprised. One day at a time.

Fabio

He came out of nowhere and effortlessly pulled his two huge suitcases out from the back of the van.

"Where are you going?" he asked, with a hint of a smile.

I hesitated for a few seconds. At first, I wasn't even sure he was talking to me, so I looked around just to be sure. Who *was* this guy? I figured he must be one of these 'brokers' that hang around at the airport and descend on 'newcomers,' aggressively offering to help them navigate through the intricacies of obtaining a flight ticket at the local airport in Lagos.

When I had arrived in Lagos about a month earlier on a different trip, a couple of these brokers methodically descended upon me like vultures. I had just bravely made it out of the international airport and was now trying to figure out how to get to Kaduna from the local airport. I was tired and mystified. There was no clear order in this local airport. I couldn't figure out where the line began and where it ended, and what for. I decided to sit down on one of the benches for a few minutes to figure things out. No sooner had I done so than two young men appeared and surrounded me.

"Auntie, where you dey go?"

"Kaduna."

"Auntie, make you sit here, make we help you get your ticket."

One of them disappeared and reappeared in a few seconds, letting me know how much the ticket would cost.

"Auntie, bring your passport. No worry, make you no stand for line – make you just sit here."

Believe it or not, I mindlessly handed them my passport only to wonder (when they had disappeared) what on earth I had just done.

Oh, Lord. Have mercy on me, Father. I can't afford to get stranded here without my passport! Help me, Lord!

"Auntie, collect your ticket," they resurfaced again with my ticket and passport intact.

I opened my mouth to express my thanks profusely when one of the two interrupted me.

"*Oya*, Auntie, make you do us weekend, a-beg."

I thanked them and tipped them. Their faces simultaneously broke into large grins.

"Auntie, thank you O. Auntie, God bless you. Auntie, make you go well, y'hear?"

I relived this scene in those seconds and decided this man had to be one of them. To his question about where I was heading, I curtly replied: "Abuja." I then reached into the back of the van, grabbed my little suitcase and rushed into the local airport. I would lose whoever he was in the mad crowd. This time, though, I could see the method to the madness. Having been here less than a month before, I knew what to do and where to go.

As I stood at the counter, getting my ticket to Abuja, I noticed someone suddenly standing beside me: the same guy with the same hint of a smile.

"Well, I'm going to Port Harcourt," he said, as if we'd been having an interesting conversation.

I looked at him and then over my shoulder, to be sure he was addressing me. He was.

"I see," I wasn't sure what to say. "I'm going to Abuja."

"You told me that already," he replied, with an amused glint in his eyes.

I was slightly embarrassed. "Oh …"

"Do you have a business card?" he asked.

"I beg your pardon?"

"Do you have a business card?"

I looked at him carefully for the first time. He had an interesting face and a severe pair of eyebrows.

I wasn't sure what to say, so I said the first thing that came to mind.

"Well, I don't live in Nigeria."

"So?" he asked.

I decided to ignore him. Maybe he would eventually just go away. The clerk at the counter, listening to this conversation, stared curiously from me to him and from him back to me.

He stood there patiently for a few more minutes, leaning against the counter with a confident little smile on his face. Finally, he said patiently, "Would you mind giving me your business card? That way I can go back and check on my children."

"Your children?"

"Yeah, I have triplets."

"*Triplets*??" I asked incredulously.

He laughed. "Yes, triplets. Three boys. Didn't you see them sitting at the other end of the airport?"

"No ..." I said apologetically.

"Didn't you notice us on the plane?" he asked.

"No," I replied honestly.

He chuckled a little, a bit embarrassed. "Well, I kept trying to catch your eye while in the plane. You walked by us a number of times."

"Oh ..." I said. Now it was my turn to be embarrassed. I wasn't used to this. I had been a married woman for fourteen years and I wasn't used to the idea of being hit on anymore. I also wasn't used to the boldness and alacrity of West African men any more. I considered the extremely casual way in which I was dressed (clearly for comfort while travelling and nothing else) and I was a bit taken aback by this uninvited attention.

After a few more minutes of waiting by me with a smile, he asked again, "May I please have your business card, if you have one?"

I gave it to him.

He called me a couple of weeks later when my trip was over and reminded me of who he was.

"I never got your name," I said.

"Fabio."

"*Fabio*?? Are you serious?"

I honestly thought he was joking and had to apologize because I realized some seconds later that my disbelief came across as rude. Okay, his name wasn't exactly 'Fabio,' but it was an Italian name that rhymed with it.

"I'm sorry," I said. "It just seems like an unusual name for an Igbo guy."

He owned a business outside the country and had just gotten divorced. He made the trip to Nigeria to get his children settled in with his mother.

"So what part of Nigeria are you from?" he asked me.

"I'm Igbo – can't you tell from my name?"

"Oh. Are you married?"

"Not anymore. If I were married, I wouldn't have given you my business card."

He laughed.

"I just got divorced, too."

We talked for a few more minutes and then he called me back some hours later. He wanted to know if I had thought about moving to Nigeria. I told him that I hadn't given it any serious thought in the last five years or so. There wasn't that much to go back to, with my father dead, and with all but one of my siblings being resident elsewhere. He urged me to begin to think about it as all that could change 'depending on how things go.'

Depending on how things go, keh?

I know our people are fast (and I admire that, living in a country where men are much 'slower'), but come *on*. Did he really think a chance meeting in an airport and a one-time phone conversation could possibly spell wedding bells?

He sent me a couple of texts later on addressing me as 'Nena-baby.' My heart sank. The instant over-familiarity was really a big turn-off for me. So was the mentality that I was just waiting for him to come along and rescue me from my status. Needless to say, the communication was short-lived. Didn't last more than a couple of days.

The nice thing about it, though, was just the shock of realizing that I'm still an attractive woman. Of course I know that (☺), but I hadn't given this any serious consideration in those early days right after my divorce.

It's still early days yet.

Thanks, Fabio. No hard feelings.

Pay attention

Several months ago, I picked up a new friend of mine on my way to see a mutual friend of ours. She needed to put something in the trunk of my car. I opened it confidently only to find it was too full of junk, and so we put her stuff in the back seat instead. "I've been carrying this junk around for the last two or three years," I mused as we drove off.

"Sometimes, the state of your car is a reflection of the state of your life," she remarked casually. I stared at her in astonishment, holding on to her words.

"Gosh, you're so right," I replied slowly.

There were actually two boxes of junk in my trunk: old parts from my car that I had replaced, but for whatever reason, I never took the time to throw out the boxes. I had always meant to. And then I just got used to carrying them around. It got to the point that I no longer really noticed them. I rarely opened the trunk of my car, anyway, so they ceased to be a real bother – or so I thought initially. But when I thought about it some more, I recalled the many times I would experience a few seconds of irritation when I went grocery shopping and had to put everything in the back seat instead of in the trunk, simply because I hadn't taken the time to discard these two boxes.

I threw the two, huge, rectangular boxes full of old car parts out of the trunk and into the trash the next morning. It felt good. I still rarely open the trunk of my car, but I feel better knowing that if I ever need to, I will find space in there for useful things.

And then, yesterday, I was talking to a good friend about my student loan. I had actually intended to pay it off two years ago. I had a solid plan for doing so, but then somehow forgot about it and instead fell into the comfortable routine of paying more than the minimum, yet not enough to knock it off in a few months like I had originally planned. "Just pay the thing off," my friend advised. "You don't want to be carrying baggage around."

I thought about it and asked myself why on earth I hadn't paid the loan off by now. I realized that the only reason under the sun was that I didn't make the time to look into my finances. I stopped paying attention and just went with the flow, without a plan. My student loan had become like a familiar friend, a buddy that I was used to having around. It was a relationship I could manage – much like a marriage – one that didn't bother me too much. I was making my monthly payments, after all, and paying substantially more than the minimum. So I had every reason to feel righteous. But I wasn't doing the best I could do. I knew I could pay it off in eight months or less without a struggle. So why hadn't I done so? I was just too busy to sit and to plan and to 'do.'

After this conversation, I resolved to pay more attention to my life. All the good intentions in the world won't help me achieve what I want to achieve. I have to *do something* to get where I want to go and stop using busyness (though I really am busy) as an excuse to not confront my life and sort out my affairs. As I thought about the student loan, I realized just how doable it was to get it over with and felt a bit ashamed that I had somehow slacked off from paying it down sooner. Again, there was no good reason. Without a plan and without action, your life will pass you by right before your very eyes. As we say in Nigeria: If you don't plan for your money (or anything else, for that matter – including relationships), other people will plan for it.

As I lie in bed this weekend, fighting off a cold and toying with the idea of working (rather than just working, like I should be), I have resolved to start finishing up my unfinished business. I'll start with my finances, and then move on to other areas of my life. I've listed four financial issues that I have to look into in order to improve my present and my future. I could ignore these areas and still get by quite alright in the short-term. But that would be pretty dumb. With just a little attention, I can make a big difference in my life.

Yesterday, I went to the bank and transferred the first batch of funds toward my eight-month goal. One month down, seven more to go.

It felt *good*.

P.S. I didn't quite achieve my eight-month goal as I originally intended. It took me nine months instead to pay the loan off in full.

Efuru and I

We Bought a Zoo.

That was the title of a movie my son watched recently. A young person from church treated him to a day out at the mall to watch a movie and have some popcorn.

"How was it?" I asked when he got back.

"Pretty good, actually," he said, and then explained it was about a father who had this grand idea of buying an old zoo to raise his children in.

What an interesting title and story, I thought.

If I had to come up with a movie title describing my family when I was growing up, it would probably be *We Bought a Library*.

I grew up surrounded by books – every kind of book imaginable on every subject imaginable. My father was a big reader and my mother is a pack-rat whose specialty was (among other things) books bought dirt cheap from libraries and garage sales. Between the two of them, we ended up with a home which looked like a library that just happened to be converted into a house.

We had no choice but to read. We spent a good portion of our lives in a small, sleepy, Nigerian town with absolutely nothing to do. There were hardly any organized activities for children at that time, and with my parents' strictness, we were rarely allowed to participate in any of them. We read because we were bored out of our minds. We had lots of fun making up our own things to do, too (don't get me wrong), but, boy, did we *read*! Even my *brothers* read (now that's how bad it was).

When my father died and I began to think a bit more clearly a few weeks later, one of the first thoughts to come to my mind was: *What's going to happen to all his books? Who's going to take care of his collection?*

My sister and I made a decision to deliberately begin to fill our homes with some of the same books we read to death – particularly, the African classics. It's kind of a competition and I think I'm losing. We update each other on the exciting (re)discoveries we've made: *Things Fall Apart; The Joys of Motherhood; The Beautyful Ones Are Not Yet Born; The People of the City; So Long a Letter; Weep Not, Child; The Lion and the Jewel; Song of Lawino; Mine Boy* ... and, of course, we both made sure we got all of Chimamanda Ngozi Adichie's books. Plus, my language studies in college opened up a whole new world of books to me, and I've been gathering a collection of the work of francophone authors that I had to read in my college days: Sembène Ousmane, Albert Camus, Mongo Béti, Aimé Césaire, Ferdinand Oyono, Ahmadou Kourouma, Frantz Fanon, Camara Laye. ...

Last year, I 'forced' my son to read *Things Fall Apart*, ignoring his initial moans, groans, and protests. I watched out of the corner of my eye as he eventually flipped open the book, and was slowly allured into the powerful story by the end of the first page. I smiled in satisfaction.

A few days later, he stormed into my room demanding to know why Okonkwo decided to commit suicide. He was disappointed, confused, frustrated, and angry even. I hid a triumphant smile and we began a long conversation about Nigerian cultures, masculinities, colonialism, and God knows what else.

An enduring love for books and reading is a gift that I hope I can leave with both of my children.

It's unusual for me to do 'hit and run' reading. I rarely ever read a book without going back to read my favorite parts of it again and again. I have read Flora Nwapa's *Efuru* a zillion times (literally) from my early teens until now, for example. Reading *Efuru* again more recently, I was struck for the first time by the parallels between her 'marriage journey' and mine.

Like me, choosing a life partner was not exactly one of Efuru's strengths. When she married Adizua, everyone wondered why. The lovey-dovey relationship eventually began to deteriorate, and Efuru had no idea why. She was the ideal wife, and had in fact married 'beneath' herself (as everyone was quick to point out behind her back). Adizua was lucky to have her and he knew it. Why did he suddenly stop worshipping the ground she walked on?

Adizua stopped eating Efuru's food. He would return home from work, and then disappear, leaving his wife to await his re-appearance for hours on end. Most times in vain. It began to affect her appetite, and she would go to bed alone. Upon his return at midnight, she would stuff her feelings of hurt, confusion, and frustration. She would welcome him as a good wife should, and offer him dinner. He would decline, saying he wasn't hungry:

'Efuru would then go to bed and think. "What is wrong?" she would ask herself. "How have I offended my husband? What am I going to do to win him back? Has he found another woman?"'

I can relate to the disappearing acts and to the sudden, inexplicable periods of moodiness. To the bending over backwards to keep the peace and to please. To having your world revolve around what you possibly could have said or done wrong this time.

Like me, Efuru had a wonderful relationship with her mother-in-law, Ossai. Ossai felt helpless as she watched Efuru's marriage to her son deteriorate for no apparent reason. She lovingly encouraged Efuru to be patient. She knew about patience and longsuffering because her own marriage had been a difficult one, and she suffered valiantly in the union during her youth. Deep down inside, though, she knew that Efuru would end up leaving her son, and she would secretly weep in anticipation of this. Efuru would listen politely to her mother-in-law's advice. Within herself, however, she would say:

'I know I am capable of suffering for greater things. But to suffer for a truant husband, an irresponsible husband like Adizua, is to debase suffering. My own suffering will be noble. When Adizua comes back, I shall leave him.'

Ossai's advice to Efuru reminds me of my own mother-in-law's words a decade ago. She also had tremendous challenges in her own marriage, and she hung in there for the long-haul, literally until the very end. She was really hoping I would do the same.

I said a short prayer and cried myself to sleep one night, confused by this dark mood that had gone on for weeks, and feeling completely helpless. In the middle of the night, I had a dream. The same old, shriveled, faceless man in a tattered top. He pointed right at me and said: "Go and read Isaiah 38: 5."

By the time I woke up, I had forgotten about the dream. My three year-old looked at me curiously that morning and asked, "Mommy, are you happy?"

"Yes, sweetie, I'm happy," I lied, surprised.

"Then how come your face is like this?" he asked, wrinkling his little face into his best frown to show me what I looked like.

"That's not how my face looks. I'm happy."

"Then smile, Mommy, smile ..." he urged.

I laughed, genuinely amused. "I'm smiling, baby, I'm smiling."

Then I remembered the dream and grabbed my Bible, turning to Isaiah 38. My eyes fell on the following words:

'This is what the Lord, the God of your father David, says: I have heard your prayer and seen your tears ...'

Stunned, I closed my Bible and sat on the bed.

My mother-in-law, who had been suspecting all was not well, said to me later that day: "Don't mind my son. Everything will be all right. God will make everything all right."

I believed her.

I was prepared to be longsuffering until the end like she was. Something snapped, though, and I changed my mind. Like Efuru, I'm prepared to suffer for some causes, but not for all.

Eneberi, Efuru's second husband, came with his own set of problems, too. They were happy enough for at least the first four years of marriage. Eventually, he went on a long-distance trading trip and did not return for months on end – not even for the burial of Efuru's father, Nwashike Ogene. Efuru worried that he might have drowned in the Great Lake. Rumor had it that he had left her:

'"What is wrong with men these days?' Ajanupu complained to [Eneberi's] mother. "You must send some people to go for your son. This is getting too much. A man like Nwashike Ogene died and Eneberi did not come home. ... What kind of trade is that? What has come over young men these days? It is disgraceful. Absolutely disgraceful. You must do something. It is humiliating. Our people are talking. Imagine Omirima saying the other day that Efuru should go and consult the dibia who will tell her why her husband has run away from her."'

What kind of trade is that? When I was married, I often asked myself what kind of business was so important that it was allowed to completely take the place of a man's family. One day, my husband returned home after six months away or more. He was distant and preoccupied. We slept side by side in the same bed like brother and sister. I wondered why he bothered to come. "I have a lot on my mind," he tried to explain. "I'm under a lot of pressure and really distracted right now. It has nothing to do with you."

What could have happened, I wondered. *Is he in trouble? Is he in debt?*

I didn't understand.

As a friend of mine said to me simply, sadly: "You didn't have a husband."

Eneberi came back from his trading trip a different man. Thin, ill, and silent. He was tight-lipped about the reason for his lengthy absence from home. The rumor circulating in the village was that Efuru's husband landed in jail while he was away on his trading trip, and it was for this reason that he stayed away for so long. Efuru was determined to find out the truth and she confronted him. He admitted that he was in jail, but denied any actual wrongdoing. Efuru demanded to know why he kept this information from her all this while. He replied:

"'I was afraid that you would be upset. It was fear only, only fear, my wife. Fear that you would desert me.'"

Four months before my divorce came through, I had an eerily similar conversation with my husband at a final family meeting. I finally asked him a question that had bugged me for years. In my mind, I had always used the metaphor of a burning house: "I just want to understand: when your house is burning down, most people instinctively dash in, grab what valuables they can, and then dash back out, satisfied that they at least managed to salvage something. In your case, you saw your house burning down before your very eyes and you acted like a casual by-stander. I don't get it. I don't understand what kind of carelessness – or arrogance, even – is behind that sort of attitude."

"It wasn't arrogance," he replied pensively. "It was fear."

There was a stunned silence in the room. None of us had expected this level of frankness. The meeting comprised several in-laws and myself. We were all too astonished, I think, to ask what exactly he meant by this.

A couple of days later, he essentially took back this remark, which irked me to no end. But I never forgot that brief moment when, for once, he felt safe enough to open up his heart and let his family have a glimpse into what was really going on in there.

On the last few pages of *Efuru*, she has a conversation with a friend, letting him know that she has left her second husband, who falsely accused her of adultery.

"'I have ended where I began – in my father's house. The difference is that now my father is dead ...'"

"I think you should consider going back to your husband."

"Difu, it is not possible. Let day break."

"Let day break, Efuru.'"

I have met many people who have tried to suggest that I get back together with my ex-husband. While I understand and appreciate this gesture, I share Efuru's conviction. Despite my own father's death, though, I do not at all feel like I've ended where I began. I'm not sure where I'm located right now, actually. But I feel more as if I'm just beginning. *Beginning what?* I wonder.

Let's see what tomorrow brings.

Let day break.

The beginning of the rest of my life

I turned 40 on a beautiful, sunny day. The agreeable weather was a nice surprise as it had been raining cats and dogs that whole month, practically.

 The last time I actually threw a birthday party, I was 21 years old. I was afraid that I would let my fortieth birthday roll by, as I'd done for years with my birthdays, without much ado. So I came up with a plan. A month or so before the day, I told the youth group at my church to plan a fortieth birthday 'bash' for me. They took up the challenge with much excitement and, in the end, I was totally blown away by what they came up with.

On the morning of my big day, I listened contentedly to the sound of young people in my living room while I made some *mean* jollof rice. The young people were laughing as they hung up balloons that popped intermittently, as they set up loudspeakers and God knows what else around the house, testing out their inventory of music for the day.

It's interesting that I turned 40 the same year I got divorced. It's also interesting to me that the year I turned 40 is the year I finally began to write.

255

I've wanted to write for as long as I can remember. Somewhere in my twenties, when I was still a young married lady, probably married for no more than two or three years, I felt a strong urge to write. I didn't, though. I was much too 'chicken.' What was I going to write about, after all? I was stumped just trying to answer that question. At the time, I felt something close to conviction for not being able to even attempt writing. Like if I had gone against or totally ignored something God had asked me to do. The feeling eventually faded over the years, though.

Then, about five or six years ago, I decided to get down to business. I was going to write if it killed me. I was going to write fiction – a simple novel that might appeal to young girls, I thought. To be fair, I did begin. My sister bought me a nice notebook and I began to fill the pages with the beginnings of my story.

Somewhere along the line, I got stuck again. I was clearly in over my head. I reprimanded myself for not mapping out the plot before starting my 'book.' Now, I was stuck with these characters that I had no idea what to do with.

This was a really bad idea, I thought to myself. Overly-ambitious. I reminded myself that my younger sister was the gifted writer of fiction in the family, not me. I was a bit confused. Why did I have such a strong desire to do something that I really wasn't equipped for in the first place? My 'work of fiction' was actually a secret from the world. No one else really knew about it except for my younger sister, and I hadn't even allowed her to read any of it. Keeping it all a secret was my safety net in case I never ended up finishing it (which, incidentally, I didn't).

And then, I was about to turn 40.

It's TRUE what they say about your forties – how your forties make you take stock of your life; how, in your forties, you begin to have a sense of having already 'paid your dues' and of no longer caring too much about what others think. I found that, as I drew closer to 40, I developed a sense of urgency over the need to do important things. With the approaching of my forties came a heightened sense of purpose, a sense that time was limited, and that whatever needed to be achieved in my life had to commence *now*. I began to have a deep aversion for doing things that clearly weren't adding value to my life – even church stuff. I no longer felt guilty about opting out of church meetings that were clearly destined to be 'boring.' I didn't want to be there if it wasn't going to add value.

Maybe I'm backsliding, I would think to myself sometimes. But I honestly wasn't interested in showing up some place to be seen or to make sure I signed a register. If I was going to be somewhere, it would have to be because I genuinely wanted to be there.

Two and a half months before I turned 40, I was in a bus filled with my work colleagues, on my way to a neighboring town, about an hour away, for a staff retreat. Half-way there, I got a call from my lawyer, telling me that my divorce had been granted.

'Thank you, thank you, thank you,' I said to him profusely.

My first sentiment was one of pure relief. As I hung up the phone, I wondered what the date was. I was startled to discover it was February 15th. I wondered if the fact that my marriage and divorce dates were identical – exactly fourteen years apart – held any significance. The relief I felt shifted into something less clear-cut. I was relieved, yes, but suddenly sad, too. It was the end of an era.

During the staff retreat, a facilitator took us through a session on developing a personal mission statement. He left the actual paperwork to get us to this goal behind with us, saying we could work on it in our spare time. I reviewed one of the forms quickly, noting that we were required to fill in the answers to a number of provocative questions. I remember two in particular because I filled in the answers to them without any hesitation. The first question asked us to list the top three people in the world that we would like to have a conversation with, if it were possible. The second asked us what we would do with our lives if money were no object – would we hold on to our current jobs, or would we do something else?

To the first question, without even a second thought, I wrote my father's name on the first line. I couldn't immediately think of the other two people in the world that I would love to have a chance to talk to. To the second question, I instantly wrote down, 'If money were no object, I would <u>write</u>.'

There, I said to myself as I put my pen down. And then I heaved a sigh of relief.

I had never been totally honest with myself about my desire to put things down on paper. I had wanted to keep a diary, for instance, for as long as I can remember – ever since I was a kid. A *real* diary where my thoughts and words would be uncensored. But I never did, for fear that someone would find it and have access to my most secret thoughts. The idea of writing just for the sake of writing had always appealed to me, but I was too afraid to admit it. I adore reading and have read a lot in my life. The idea of attempting to 'join' those whose work I've read and admired by attempting to write myself just seemed plain ridiculous. But that day, I finally allowed myself to think this thought.

My sister and I talked about this recently and I told her that I finally get why it was always so hard for me to write for pleasure. I had never thought outside the fiction box. My sister writes fiction effortlessly, and I just assumed that this is what I would write, too. I thought that this had to be my genre, too. What else was there to write about, I wondered?

After the retreat, I realized that I was going to write about the only thing I really knew well – my life.

I started writing one weekend in March. I sat down in my kitchen (in between making some *okazi* soup) and wrote. And wrote. And wrote.

I'm just going to write, I told myself – *no matter what, no matter how it sounds, no matter how 'imperfect' it might be. I'm just going to write about the only thing I know. I'll write about whatever comes to me, whenever it comes.* The more I wrote, the more I realized I had something to write about. I had something important to say and I was going to write it down and hope it would one day be found by someone that really needed to hear it.

The year I got divorced is the year I turned 40, and the year in which my attention was drawn to Micah 6: 5b: 'Remember your journey from Shittim to Gilgal,' it says in the NIV, 'that you may know the righteous acts of the Lord.'

To try and 'spice up' my Bible reading that year, I decided to start reading the Old Testament backwards – from Malachi to Genesis (weird, I know). In the process, I stumbled upon Micah 6: 5 and then began to explore the circumstances that led God to give this instruction. I meditated on Micah 6: 5 and what I had learned for a week.

The following week, I was in a hospital room for two nights with my daughter, who had been admitted. The TBN channel was on. I hadn't watched TBN in quite a while and was happy to have it on in the background, though I wasn't paying it any attention. As I sat on the hospital bed searching for something in my purse, Rod Parsley's authoritative voice boomed at me: "DO YOU KNOW WHAT GILGAL MEANS?" he asked, tauntingly.

I dropped my purse and looked up at the TV with my mouth open.

"'Gilgal' means 'axle'," he continued. "Gilgal is the place of your *turn-around*!" And with that, he proceeded to turn around on his heel in his dramatic, Parsley-esque fashion.

"*Halleluia*!!!" I yelled back at him impulsively with all my might. And then I peeped sheepishly outside the window, hoping I hadn't disturbed the peace too much.

On my fortieth birthday, when an old family friend of ours was asked to pray for me, he made a reference to Gilgal during his prayer. *There it is again*, I said to myself.

As I write this morning, I'm looking at Joshua 5: 9, which says: 'Then the Lord said to Joshua, "Today I have rolled away the reproach of Egypt from you. So the place has been called **Gilgal** to this day.'" Interestingly, this pronouncement was made after the Israelites had wandered about in the desert for forty years.

In a word, I entered into my fortieth year with gratitude, with wonder, with genuine excitement. I danced my heart out on my birthday, surrounded by true friends, as well as by the laughter, dancing, and joyful shrieks of young people. I danced before the Lord until my hair was literally drenched with sweat, looking like I'd just stepped out of a swimming pool.

The Lord has been good to me. My whole life, I've been blessed. And as for this 'bump in the road' that my divorce represents along my blessed journey – I will go over it gracefully, and I will come out on the other side, giving glory and honor to the God who was my ever-present rear guard, my buckler, my rampart, my help, and my shield along the way.

I've been here before

I made one of my first major, frightening, life-changing decisions at the age of 17.

After a full year of studying Chemistry at the University, I decided to change my major to French. I knew my father would kill me, so I set things in motion behind his back. I found my first year at the University academically boring. By the second term, I knew there was no way I could go through four years of it. The classes were so large and unwieldy that I barely knew what my lecturers looked like. But that wasn't the real problem. I was bored to death and not performing well for the first time in my life, but that wasn't the problem, either. I just knew that this couldn't be where my life was supposed to be headed. There had to be more to life than this.

As I approached each lecturer in the Languages Department to sign the necessary forms permitting me to change my major, they were all terrified. My father sat on the senate and was essentially their superior. "Is he aware of this? Had he endorsed this?" they wanted to know before signing. The Head of Department wanted to know why my father hadn't personally approached him to discuss this. I found a polite way of saying that my father already had his degrees, and that this was about me now.

I look back with wonder at that time, given that I'm one of the most indecisive people I know. I was propelled by a *knowing* that I was on the wrong path. Naturally, all hell broke loose when my family found out, but I'll skip over that part. The bottom line is that everyone eventually learned to live with it.

"Don't think this is going to be easy," a lecturer in the Languages Department warned me as she eyed me coldly from head to toe. "You've missed a whole year of French, remember. Don't think your father's presence in this university will make things any easier for you here."

My eyes smarted with tears and I blinked them away.

My father relayed the same message. It wasn't necessarily going to be any easier. In life, you don't run away from your problems. *I'm not running away*, I would say to myself. *I'm just doing what feels right. Chemistry feels totally wrong.* I was frightened – scared to death, actually – but I was much more scared of ending up at the wrong destination in the future.

For good measure, my father opted not to buy my text books for the next couple of years. I took it all in stride. After attending my very first French class, I knew everything would be alright. I began truly enjoying learning again. I borrowed pretty much all my books from a lecturer in the English Department, a family friend of my parents, who happened to have almost every book I needed. It was our secret pact.

Three years later, I graduated at the top of my class. I defended my thesis before a panel which included the lecturer that had essentially predicted doom when I first transferred to the department. She interrupted the session to say that she had been keeping track of my progress over the years and was both surprised by and proud of the outcome. She talked about how she still remembered the first day I arrived. The Head of Department interrupted her, asking her to save her sentiments for after my defense.

I smiled on the inside.

I didn't attend my graduation as I had left the country by then. My father did, though, and others in attendance tell me that when my name was announced as the departmental prize-winner, my father jumped up and exclaimed: *"That's my daughter!"*

Years later, I had a cross-country phone conversation with my father. It was November 16th. I was heavily pregnant and complained to him about not having seen my then husband in eight months. "Don't worry. You'll be alright," my father said. "You're a strong girl. All my daughters are strong women."

Strong? I wondered. How unusual for anyone to use such a word to describe me. There are definitely strong women in my family, but I have never considered myself to be one of them.

Little did I know that this was to be the last conversation I would have with my father. My daughter was born on November 29th and my father was gone – tragically snatched away – about a week later.

I don't think any of us thought we would survive it. I don't think anyone thought *I* would survive it. My eldest brother broke the news to me on the phone, with his wife on the other line. They held their breath, waiting for the meltdown. I took deep breaths, mumbled something, and hung up with the tears stinging my eyes. My husband waited for the meltdown, confused by my stillness and calmness.

In my usual fashion, I did my crying in small, deep increments. In the bathroom. In the bedroom. In the car. Always alone.

I still cry.

If I could deal with my father's death – if I am still here and of sound mind years later – then surely I can handle anything.

"You're *very* strong emotionally," a friend of mine said on the phone last month. I have known this friend since I was 11 years old. We went to the same secondary school and became tight friends when I was probably about 14. Her comment surprised me and reminded me of my father's.

I haven't seen her since I was 16. What gave her this conviction isn't at all clear to me. I look back at my life between the ages of eleven and sixteen and cannot imagine what she saw during those years to convince her of my emotional strength in particular. But these days, I need all the strength I can get, and so I've chosen to believe her. And to believe my father.

After a decade in the U.S. and years of trying to find my way back to the African continent, I got an interesting-sounding job and decided to take the leap. "Everyone else is trying to move to the U.S. Why would you want to go back to Africa?" people would say.

I guess I'm just not everyone else. I had never been to this part of the continent, but I just knew it was the right move for me. "People want to hire you here. Are you sure this is what you want to do?" my boss at the time asked.

After going through a period of uncertainty, I suddenly had two similar job offers in the US. But when I got a similar offer in Africa, I instinctively knew which one I was supposed to take. I was sure. I had been here before. I had been in this difficult place where the most obvious decision was not the right decision for me.

And so I relocated without looking back. Almost a decade later, I have no regrets – and if I had to do it all over again, I would make the same decision. Those that once wondered why on earth I would want to relocate have since understood.

With my divorce, therefore, I find myself in familiar territory. It's a weird spot to be in, not knowing what the future holds. But if my whole life has been anything to go by, I know I'll be alright.

I can do this.

Without Crutches

My tent is destroyed; all its ropes are snapped. ... [N]o one is left now to pitch my tent or to set up my shelter (Jeremiah 10: 20, NIV).

When it comes to reading the Bible, I may just have attention deficit disorder.

I mean, I like to read it (some days more than others – like on weekends when I can really focus), and I do read it regularly. There are periods of time when I'm hungry for the Word and reading it isn't a struggle. For the most part, though, I have to devise strategies in order to ensure that I remain a regular reader, and that I don't get bored in the process. I'm always trying to come up with new ways of doing this.

I'm not good with devotionals. I admire people that can read *Our Daily Bread* day after day, year after year. My sister is one of them. I would just go crazy. I've tried a range of devotionals and finally just had to accept that I'm not a devotional person. I can't manage following a devotional for more than 2-3 days straight. I have a couple lying around in case I ever feel like using one, but I usually just decide which book of the Bible I'm going to focus on and then read it bit by bit until I'm done. Or focus on a particular topic for a while. I do *really like* Rick Warren's

Purpose Driven Connection devotionals, though. They pop into my inbox once or twice a day and they're always really inspiring and practical; so much so that I am actually considering trying devotionals one more time.

This morning, I started out reading a *Purpose Driven Connection* devotional but then started looking up something else (like I said, A.D.D.!), and then somehow stumbled on John 5: 8 which says: 'Pick up your mat and walk.'

I was riveted by this command and forgot all about the devotional I was supposed to be reading. I decided to focus on John 5: 1-11 instead (some verses edited here to ensure brevity):

'Sometime later, Jesus went up to Jerusalem. Now there is in Jerusalem a pool called Bethesda. Here, a great number of disabled people used to lie – the blind, the lame, the paralyzed.'

I stopped and thought: Wait a minute. What are *my* **disabilities**? What are those things that send me a message about what I'm supposedly not **able** to do? Are there certain things that I'm simply not **able** to see (blind), or walk toward (lame)? Or am I simply paralyzed (by fear, for instance) even though my limbs seem okay?

'Here, a great number of disabled people used to lie …'

How come the disabled were all lying together? Hanging out with each other? Where was everybody else? I asked myself if I needed to change the company I currently keep.

Well, Bethesda was a healing pool, so I suppose it made sense for those that needed healing to hang around it and, therefore, around each other. But still. I wondered if any of their lives would have been different had they integrated with people that were **able** to do what they could not.

The company I keep is small. Too small, frankly. I'm comfortable with the company I keep, but comfort isn't everything. I do realize I need to widen my network. To let even more people into my world. Even more people that will inspire me and stretch my cap*abilities*. In other words, it's not always about getting rid of your old friends. Sometimes, it's just about making room for the new, too.

'One who was there had been an invalid for thirty-eight years. When Jesus saw him lying there and learned that he had been in this condition for a long time, he asked him, "Do you want to get well?"'

This question from Jesus never fails to rattle me, no matter how many times I read this story.

I'm the sort of person that is naturally given to self-pity (yeah, I'll admit it). I noticed this trait in my early teens, was absolutely horrified by it, and have fought it tooth and nail ever since. I have had great success in overcoming most of it, but remnants are still there. I'm very lucky that I'm too busy to throw any kind of party. This has really helped in mitigating any self-pity I might have otherwise wallowed in over the last few years. I simply don't have the time. And so when I do begin to sink into that patch of quicksand, I quickly scramble out. There's just far too much to do, so I put that appointment with myself on the backburner.

To be fair to this 38 year-old man, he had been in this condition, in this state of inertia, 'for a long time.' My first inclination, personally, would have been to express sympathy. And so it startles me how Jesus cuts straight to the chase and gets to the core of the issue: 'Do you *want* to get well?'

Appearances can be deceptive. Sometimes, everything is not quite as it seems. Boy, does this underscore the importance of introspection! What do I really *want*?

I'm finding that it takes time and reflection to respond to this seemingly simple question.

What do I want from now on – *and how badly do I want it*? What sort of effort do I need to invest to get it? How prepared am I to invest the level of effort required? Do I *really* want what I want, or is that just rhetoric?

'"Sir," the invalid replied, "I have no one to help me into the pool when the water is stirred. While I am trying to get in, someone else goes down ahead of me."'

Another thing that never ceases to amaze me is how this man totally avoided answering the simple question. And yet, I can relate. It's hard to dig down into yourself, bring up the truth, and stare it in the eye.

Even healing can be scary.

Everyone else around assumes an 'invalid' should want to be healed … but does one really?

Change can be scary. Success can be scary. Accepting the fact that your miracle is obtainable can be scary. Achieving your dreams can be scary. Knowing that we can actually get what we want can sometimes be the most frightening thing on earth. I suppose that's what Marianne Williamson meant. If we really took the time to analyze our fears, we would be shocked by what we're *really* afraid of.

Do I really want to move on? *Of course*, is my automatic, knee-jerk reply.

But what does 'moving on' mean?

A list of clichés. Starting from scratch. Learning new rules. (Caring that new rules might even exist.) Putting myself out there. Stepping into the unknown.

It's easier to just stay where I am. To just get by. To not dream again. To allow my day-to-day life's momentum to just carry me wherever, with no vision for where I actually want to end up.

Do I want to get well?

'Then Jesus said to him, "Get up! Pick up your mat and walk." At once the man was cured; he picked up his mat and walked.'

Whoa!

"Get up" with an exclamation mark! Still a bit too 'harsh' of a command for my own sensibilities. The man was an 'invalid' for goodness sake! And not only 'GET UP,' but 'PICK UP YOUR MAT AND WALK.'

I paused again. What was this 'mat' about? Wouldn't it have been enough if he just got up? That was the actual miracle after all … right?

And then it hit me.

My 'mat' is my crutch. It's the crutch that lets my 'disability' rest and feel comfortable. It represents all my excuses for not getting up and moving forward. In picking up my mat, therefore, I do two things: I leave myself with nowhere to 'lie' around anymore, and I show myself that I am bigger than that which I thought I needed support from.

Until you validate yourself, you will remain an invalid.

No excuses – no matter how compelling they sound.

No more crutches.

Note: This chapter has focused on my own symbolic 'disabilities' that I think I can actually do something about. There are many people living with real disabilities of all kinds, and the chapter is not written from that perspective, nor is it suggesting that the solutions offered here can or should apply to them.

No Weapon

S he came into my bedroom with a strange expression on her face. It's hard to accurately describe what the expression was like. I had never seen it on her face before, and this was a face that I knew well.

It was an expression of *longing*.

At least that's what it looked like to me. The expression matched the tone of her text messages, which I had ignored until she gave up. I remember thinking how odd this was – the stream of text messages which repeatedly affirmed how much she missed me and our friendship. I mean, I know I make a great friend (if I do say so myself). I was definitely good to her and, to be honest, she was good to me, too. But I tried to put myself in her shoes and I was convinced that if a good friend of mine accused me of sleeping with her husband, that would spell the end of the friendship (whether the accusation were true or not). There are so many potential friendships to be cultivated in this world that it would not be worth it to me to continually pursue a friend that believed I would do that to her. Or if the accusation were true, I would rather make myself scarce than go through the motions of trying to keep the friendship alive.

She came in dressed in a casual top – a t-shirt, maybe – and a wrapper. I was lying in bed with a slight tummy ache and watched as she walked toward me with this weird facial expression, telling me again how much she missed our friendship. And with that, she laid right next to me. She immediately began complaining about having a tummy ache, too – a serious one. She actually began writhing in pain. And then she told me she was bleeding. I jumped out of bed and grabbed a sanitary pad to hand to her only to discover she didn't have any underwear on – just the wrapper. I also realized that this was not a menstrual problem, given the sheer volume of blood that had gushed out. She had bled profusely onto the bed sheets. I managed to strip them off the bed before the blood stained the mattress, carrying a large volume of blood in the sheets. And then I immediately woke up, shivering and with an eerie feeling.

It was at that point that it dawned on me that whether I realized it or not, whether I completely understood it or not, whether I liked it or not, I was in the midst of a spiritual battle.

I said I 'woke up,' but in actual fact, I wasn't quite sleeping. I was in a place or state that is between sleep and wakefulness. And I 'snapped out of it' as soon as I rescued my mattress from blood stains.

I had a number of these odd 'encounters' in the very early days before I had made up my mind to file for divorce. I want to lay the memories of these particular encounters to rest once and for all. There are some things that I have not had to think twice about writing about. And then there are a few other things that I have decided do not need to be said. Until now, this has been one of those things. I finally decided to write about this now because it occurred to me that when a covenant is broken, we usually privilege certain aspects of the tragedy (say, the emotional or social or financial aspects) over other components. There is a spiritual dimension that we rarely hear about – or that I personally had hardly heard about until I experienced it myself.

This is one of the things I wish I could let my former spouse know. Through no fault of my own, I was suddenly thrown into a dark battle that I did not fully understand, and I was left with a big mess to sort out and clean up.

She came into my room again on another night. I was lying in bed, neither completely asleep nor completely awake. This time, she walked in and lay directly on top of me. Then she forced her face all the way into mine and ended this process by jutting her chin directly into mine. I snapped out of it and began to plead the *Blood of Jesus* and pray fervently.

In addition to these weird encounters, I had a number of dreams that month. Other members of my household were having bad dreams, too. I realized at this point that things were getting out of hand and that I needed to be more aggressive in my approach. This was not child's play.

Out came my anointing oil. I went around the house like a high priestess, binding and casting, taking authority, praying the Scriptures, and anointing every room, along with my marital bed. A close family friend came over and shared the Scriptures and prayed with me as well.

After that night, everyone's bad dreams ceased.

In the midst of all this commotion, God was there, too. He was *there*. Again, this was in the very early days and I was still in the throes of grief. I would lie under the covers in my bedroom after work and suddenly just feel God's presence in the room with me. Quiet. Present. *There.*

I did not 'hear' anything, but I knew He was with me. I strongly sensed that I was not alone and I was comforted. He was respectful of my grief and I did not feel any pressure to do anything in particular, or to be anything in particular, or to make any decisions in particular.

I had one more 'dream.' Fortunately, I document my dreams (all the ones that I remember) as soon as I wake up and email them to myself so I can review them again if I ever need to. Once again, it wasn't really a dream as I wasn't asleep, but I wasn't exactly awake, either.

I was lying in bed that night when two women entered my room. I remember being struck by how well-dressed they were. They looked really sophisticated and classy and were dressed in business-like skirt suits. They were extremely well-coiffed and were both carrying briefcases. They sat on the edge of my bed and began telling me things. I couldn't remember exactly what they had said, but it had to do with my life and the experiences I had had during these very early stages. They had such insight into what I'd been through that I started weeping. I cried so hard that when I actually 'woke up,' my eyelashes were stuck together and it took me a while to pry my eyes open.

When I was done crying, one of them opened her briefcase and brought out a wad of notes.

'Here's a thousand dollars,' she said. 'Your husband gave this to [The Strange Woman]. It rightfully belongs to you.'

I took it, in shock.

I then asked the two women a question. Something like, "How did you know all this?"

Their response gave me the chills. They answered: *"Do you not know that there are angels in the corporate world?"* This response stayed with me, ringing in my ears long after I had woken up.

I didn't quite understand what they meant.

The next thing I knew, I was transferred to another scene in this 'dream.' There was this huge auditorium. I peeped inside and then decided to sneak in and sit at the very back, in the dark, where I would go unnoticed. There was a high table with some managers sitting around it, while most people sat in the auditorium seats. I sat there listening to the deliberations and realized I was in a meeting of the company that my former friend worked for. It was a long meeting, but in summary, the deliberations gave me insight into things that I had only suspected but did not know for sure. As this corporate meeting drew to a close, one of the managers at the high table voiced the collective decision of the senior management. The decision was to fire my former friend. As he began to announce this decision, I remember being horrified. According to my typed up notes of that dream from five years ago, I said in the dream, *'Oh, no! God, no. Please don't let her get fired. She has so many financial responsibilities and her whole family depends on her ... Lord, no. Please don't let that happen.'*

I was transferred back into my bedroom with the two well-coiffed women still sitting on the edge of my bed. They said some more things which I do not remember. When they left, their earlier words kept ringing in my ears: *Do you not know that there are angels in the corporate world?*

It was only upon their departure that I realized they were also trying to tell me they were actually angels themselves.

I know it sounds 'spooky' and out-of-this-world. It does, even for me. I'm not a 'spooky' person, but I cannot deny that this happened, and that this is my understanding of the incident.

When I ran into my former friend some time later and she mentioned she'd been fired from her job, I remembered this dream/non-dream and went back to review what I had documented.

Back then, I was not interested in vilifying my former, dear friend. Five years later, I'm even less interested in doing so. I'm more invested in the idea of standing in awe of God for His faithfulness through the years, and for delivering me from whatever He delivered me from. For delivering Totally-Clueless-Me.

I don't fully know or understand what went on. I have accepted that I may never fully understand. I prefer to blame some of these things on the spirit behind people than on the people themselves. Otherwise, it all gets much too confusing. I think that if my ex-husband had had deeper insight into the kind of trouble he was inviting into our home, into his life, into mine, and into our children's lives, he just might've thought twice. The deception lies in thinking it's all about you and that it's not hurting anyone else.

I haven't thought about these incidents in a long time, but at this moment, I'm reminded of how much I have to be thankful for.

No weapon formed against me shall prosper (Isaiah 54:17, NKJV).

Healing

I have not written a single word in months, and, strangely enough, I have not felt compelled to.

It certainly hasn't been for a lack of things to write about. Admittedly, there are fewer things now to get out of my system than there were a year ago when I started writing. But there are still 'things,' nonetheless. As I started doing a year ago, I still maintain a list of bullet points – titles, phrases, sentences, or partial sentences just waiting to be elaborated upon and written up into complete memoir pieces. Today, there are six bullet points on the list, to be exact, drawn up over the past several months.

But I find that I am bored by my own list. Events that have occurred recently, which at one time would have been fodder for a write-up, now appear 'stale' somehow. My silence for the last six weeks has not been a reflection of the fact that nothing has transpired, but rather of the fact that I no longer find these events remarkable.

I thought to myself the other day: *This must be what healing feels like.*

Not the instant-miracle-type healing. But the conventional kind – the kind where you feel every bit of the pain … until you don't. The kind that is by the every day, banal sort of faith. You know: the sort of faith that gets you up every morning and makes you keep moving, get through the day, and prepare for the next – not knowing exactly what tomorrow holds, but figuring that as long as you're alive and breathing without medical assistance (and even if you aren't), you are operating in a context of possibilities – anything can happen. Convinced that as long as you have a precious, precious life, you might as well live it and use it.

It hasn't been the 'sudden healing' type of experience. I have felt everything I needed to feel. I have been busy raising and trying to organize the lives of two children – each at very different stages of development, and both growing in every way at an incredible pace; busy surviving in a non-profit career world with less funding than ever and more responsibilities and pressure as a result; busy trying to contribute in my own little way to ensuring that my church home thrives and is a refuge for others while remaining meaningful for me, too; busy trying to identify and invest in things that will help take care of me when I'm no longer young enough and strong enough to work as hard as I do now.

With all this activity and more, it's understandable that I'm sometimes caught off guard when I'm hit by a sudden pang of grief, provoked for a few seconds by some random memory. I do not live my life wallowing in grief and so I'm usually unprepared for this unexpected visitor. I'm usually surprised that this tiny pang is powerful enough to penetrate the many layers of my life and make me actually notice.

But feeling a pang or two now and then is part of the healing process, I think – a sign of some serious progress, even. (It's a pang now and then, as opposed to the full-blown waves I used to experience.) Sort of like when a scab begins to form over an open wound. The tightness of the scab causes twinges of pain initially, but the pain is no less a sign that some major healing processes have occurred, and that the end is in sight. The scab will eventually give way to nature, loosen up, and then disappear. There might always be reminders of the wound, though, just like an indelible mark from a wound that has healed will always serve as a reminder. I suppose it's a lot like the kind of healing I have gradually experienced in regard to my father's death. It is still deeply painful to think about it, but thinking about it does not practically incapacitate me like it would have six years ago. I have not 'forgotten' and I do not want to forget. But I can say that I am as 'healed' from that experience as I will ever be. Despite this healing, I will always carry a considerable amount of the pain with me. And I welcome this pain because I always unabashedly treasured and always will unabashedly treasure my father.

In the same way, I welcome these unexpected pangs of pain now and then. They remind me that I was once part of something that was meant to be really special – a deep, *deep* covenant. Before I got married, I always treasured the idea of marriage, having no inkling of what it could potentially involve. During my marriage, I treasured the reality of (my own particular) marriage, believing that two people on the same page could conquer the world, even if my spouse and I were not. Post-marriage, I still treasure the notion of a *real* marriage. I do so unabashedly.

I look back now and I am proud of the twenty-something-year-old me who – ignorant and naïve as she was – dared to dream and enter into marriage with all her heart. I am proud of the thirty-something-year-old me who found the courage to face some hard truths about her life, and to make a distinction between a dream and a nightmare. I am proud of the lessons I have gleaned – the forty-something-year-old me – older, wiser, and more alive now than I have ever been in my adult life.

I have learned that divorce is a lot like a chronic illness: It needs to be managed.

It's always with you and you are never 100 percent free from it, but if you manage it properly, you will barely notice it most days. Discovering you have a chronic illness can be utterly devastating, but how you turn out in the end is really up to you, oftentimes. The diagnosis can be the defining moment that leads to death, or it can instead be the critical incident that grants one a new lease on life. Being diagnosed with a chronic illness can often mean that self-care suddenly becomes paramount. It can provide the impetus for one to finally pay attention to oneself and inculcate healthy behaviors that we know we should practice, but tend to ignore. It leaves one with the sudden realization that today is a gift and tomorrow is not promised.

Similarly, as devastating as divorce is, it does not have to mean death. It can be managed properly, to the point that you forget most of the scars, and begin to look forward to living a full life, despite your 'condition.'

If this is what healing feels like, then it isn't half bad.

AFTERWORD

*The light shines in the darkness, and the darkness can never
extinguish it (John 1:5, NLT).*

I have come to the end.

Not the end of remembering, as most of my memories will
probably always remain with me. But I have come to the end
of that which I have felt the need to tell.

On occasion, I have questioned the utility of sharing my
memories in the form of a book. About a year before writing
these final words, some dear friends of mine (a married couple)
made me pause and explore my motives for moving forward
with this publication. Their intention was not to discourage
me, but to simply play devil's advocate – just to be sure that I
was clear about things in my own mind. "Having a blog is one
thing," they said. "But having a book is a whole other ball game.
Why did you write this book?"

I wrote this book because I was meant to write it. My mind
is simply unable to accept the notion that my experiences in
marriage and divorce have no purpose. There is a reason for the

path that I have walked, and this book represents one piece of that puzzle.

I wrote this book because when I was struggling in a difficult marriage, and then, navigating the waters of divorce, I desperately yearned to read about the experience of others to help me with mine, and I couldn't find any books by anyone like me.

I wrote this book because the reactions to what began simply as a blog made me realize there is a need for it – not just for the divorced, but for the married and never-married as well. I have written frankly about quite a number of things that I wish someone had been able to articulate for me before I got married. I have written about things I wish I had known when I was in a marriage. Through this book, I have also attempted to put the dark areas of marriage (some marriages, anyway), and of divorce under a spotlight. In my mind, there is no better way to stem the tide of stigma than to 'turn on the lights,' so to speak.

In many ways, stigma is incredibly unoriginal: It really doesn't matter what it's attached to – its workings are predictable and consistent: There's always the fear first. We're naturally afraid of that which we know little or nothing about – of that which we have not experienced ourselves. Self-protection is therefore an immediate and understandable priority. We're not sure whether the stigmatized condition or circumstance is 'catching' – and if it is, we want to ensure that we do not succumb to the contagion.

Plus, there is the fear of delving into the unknown. We are afraid of what we might learn. Consequently, we would rather not take the time search the issue out. After all, *what if that which we learn changes us?* Change can be so hard to stomach. We are already neatly-packaged (or so we would like to believe) and we would rather not experience any unravelling of our neatly-packaged selves. It's too much trouble.

Until, of course, the issue touches us personally.

Usually, it is only then that we begin to do our due diligence – to leave no stone unturned in just trying to at least *understand*.

My personal experience has been that discussions about divorce in the Church in Africa are unceremoniously hushed up on the rare occasion when they do commence. This is closely related to fear and to the erroneous notion that side-stepping an issue erases its existence. And since fear is always coupled with underdevelopment, there is a lack of tools for dealing with divorce in the Africa-based Church, as well as a lack of appropriate language for talking about it. The time it takes to develop these essential tools has simply not been invested.

But we need to understand that discussions about divorce involve far more than just divorce alone. Discussions about divorce are necessarily discussions about *marriage*. They are about how to prepare potential marrieds. They are about how to bolster current, struggling marrieds. They are about what can go wrong, what to look out for, what to avoid, what to work on. They are, in a sense, more 'honest' than most current marriage-based discussions because there are raw and naked and open. Divorce experiences, tragic as they may be, are a *resource*.

As often is the case with endings, bringing this book to an end gives me a slight anti-climactic feeling: *Well, who cares? So what if my marriage ended? Of what use is this anatomy of a marriage and divorce now that it has been carried out?*

In response to that feeling, I will say that I think women might care. Whatever the state of one's marriage, I think the anatomical procedure that this book represents will prompt women to sit up and begin to consider preventive measures lest my reality – God forbid – becomes theirs.

I think men might care. Because communication is often such a huge problem in marriage, my impression is that many men have no inkling of just what kind of pain certain actions can inflict on their partners. I hope that many of the chapters in this book will give them a glimpse into just what it is like – a glimpse into just how much havoc a poor decision made in a split second can cause.

I think the Church might care. My one-time marriage represents just one of many African, Christian marriages hanging by a thread or already destroyed. I hope that my laying it all out will obligate the Church in Africa to view the remains of one marriage (mine), and glean something from the autopsy in order to help other struggling marriages. I hope that the Church will gain a sense of how to better provide support, and of actions to take in general, by reading my story.

Why did I write this book? I wrote this book as a memorial of what I regard as an extremely important journey. As the Scriptures promise, in 'remembering my journey,' I have come to understand more keenly the righteous acts of God in my life despite the catastrophe of divorce. I hope that this account of my journey will inspire others going through divorce to look for the gems along the way – for there are gems to be found. I am in absolute *awe* of what God has been able to bring me through.

My head is up. I am navigating today successfully, and I am ready for the new dawn of tomorrow.

Ka chi fo.